Be Great:

Lessons Learned from a Life in the Dirt

ABOUT THE AUTHOR

Charles Schultz grew up in Worthington, Ohio. He spent the majority of his youth playing sports which took him to Youngstown State University on a baseball scholarship. As a college athlete Charles became an All-American and was a member of the first conference championship in school history. Following a successful playing career Charles began to give back through coaching and training.

In 2020 Charles began to The Edge of Greatness Project which sparked the desire to share this story with everyone. Charles now lives in Wooster, Ohio with his wife Erin and three children Hunter, Sayler, and Charlotte (Charlie). He spends most of his days coaching and working on becoming a better leader.

Charles has spent several years writing different stories, blogs, and articles. Be Great: Lessons Learned From a Life in the Dirt is his first nonfiction work. To see what Charles is doing next please visit www.charlesaschultz.com.

Connect with Charles
Facebook @charlesaschultz1983
Instagram @coach_schultz7

www.charlesaschultz.com

Be Great:

Lessons Learned from a Life in the Dirt

Charles Schultz

BE GREAT

Visit the author at www.charlesaschultz.com

Printed in the United States of America

ISBNs: 978-1-972291-00-9 (paperback), 978-1-972291-01-6 (hardcover), 978-1-972291-05-4 (ebook)

SPECIAL THANKS

I believe we are a product of the people we're surrounded by. I've been incredibly blessed to have some absolutely incredible people make an impact on my life. If I were to thank everyone it would take me an entire book. Many of the people who have shaped me are mentioned in this book, but I want to give a special thanks to Chuck and Cyndi Schultz (my parents). Through their love and support I've been able to take on the various challenges my life has presented and become stronger. My beautiful wife Erin and my three kids Charles Hunter, Sayler, and Charlotte. Without your love and support I wouldn't be able to pursue my dreams and be who I am today. I'm so happy to be able to share this journey with you. All the coaches, teachers, students, clients, and athletes who have taught me so much about myself and what it means to pursue greatness. Thank you all so much.

CONTENTS

Dedication to Coach Stephen Gussler

As I was writing this book and recalling several stories and memories of my life, I kept being reminded of how incredible my journey has been. I've been blessed in so many ways, but one of the most incredible blessings I received was the opportunity to play and learn from my high school baseball coach, Stephen Gussler. His leadership and tutelage are a big part of why I am the man I am today. He was an inspiration to an entire community during his life, and that impact will be felt forever. I'm going to include a Facebook post I wrote during his battle with cancer that I felt the world needed to see. Many of the stories in this initial post that I made back in 2014 will appear again throughout this book, as they are lessons learned from a man who led a life full of greatness.

When growing up, I was often told that the Lord never asks more of us than what we are capable of handling. I guess it makes sense, then, that Coach Stephen Gussler has been asked to do so much. There is no doubt that the Lord knows there is no stronger man to carry such an incredible torch. His fight with cancer has been long and oftentimes seemingly insurmountable, yet his courage and constantly upbeat and positive attitude have inspired so many. Even through pain, bad news, and unfortunate circumstances, Coach Guss has pushed forward.

While I have not had the opportunity to be around Coach Guss as much in recent years, his bravery and teachings still guide me today. It is because of this that I wish to share with everyone a few stories I have of the most caring, demanding, courageous, fair, and inspiring leader I've had the privilege to know.

I first met Coach Gussler when I was in eighth grade. He was finishing his first season as the varsity head coach at Thomas Worthington High School. I was too old to play summer travel ball, so instead I played with the high school team. We didn't interact a whole lot in that first summer, but the few times he did make an appearance at the games, I could tell the respect he had already earned from my teammates.

That following year is when I truly began to see who Coach Gussler really was. He was a competitor. Challenging his players at every turn, but doing so while participating himself in the drills. It was a unique approach that I had never had before. Every ground ball, every pop fly, every swing off the tee, and every sprint, Coach Guss was there pushing to get the most out of us. He loved the hard work, he loved to push and challenge us, but most of all, he loved to compete, and it was that which rubbed off on his players the most.

No matter what the odds or how far down we were, we competed. Whether it was the top of the first or the bottom of the seventh, we competed. If we were down eight or up ten, our effort never wavered and we competed. Still today when you watch a Coach Gussler-coached team, you see that competitiveness emerge. Even though Coach Gussler is no longer able to compete at practice the way he once did, his ability to show up each day and compete against a much greater foe inspires his team the same, perhaps even more.

That same year I was lucky enough to make the varsity team as a freshman. At the time I didn't know what an honor that was and really wanted to play travel basketball with my friends along with baseball. I remember going into his office and asking him to play AAU (which is the governing body of travel basketball) during the season, telling him it wouldn't interfere with any practices or games. He of course told me no, sending me home so upset that I wanted to quit baseball. I mean, obviously, a five-foot-eleven power forward is destined for the NBA.

I was talked off the ledge by my mom, thankfully, and returned to practice the next day ready to commit 100 percent to baseball. My commitment to baseball was returned by Coach Gussler's commitment to me. During that first season, he showed me baseball, which was my first love, is where I truly belonged. Teaching me more in one season than I had learned in fourteen years prior, he also believed in me so much that he got me to move from the outfield to shortstop.

In that first season I also learned the value of committing fully to whatever you're doing at the time. Too often people participate in something half-heartedly. We say we want something, but in turn don't put forth the necessary effort to achieve it. Coach Gussler is a person who commits 100 percent to the thing he's involved in. That commitment to whatever he's doing at the time ensures that he always gives his very best. It's a rare quality, and one that I still strive for today.

I know that playing varsity at such a young age probably didn't sit well with all the parents, especially those whose kid's spot I was taking. Yet, even through my struggles, Coach Guss stayed with me, pushing me at the right times and building me up when necessary. His ability to coach is unparalleled, always able to get the most out of all his players no matter what their personality and ability. This is rare because he knew when to yell, when to teach, when to motivate, and how to get everyone to buy in all the time.

One of my favorite moments that I still remember as clearly as the day it happened reflects just how well he knows his players, especially how well he knew me. I was playing shortstop, and there was a runner on second base with two outs. The batter hit a hard shot into the hole between second and third. I took three hard steps diving to my right, the ball sticking into my glove right along the edge of the outfield grass. Then, being the all-star that I thought I was, I popped up onto my knees (planning to make a throw across the diamond from my knees), reached into my glove and bobbled the ball.

The ball fell to the ground harmlessly and all the runners were safe. While my dive saved the run, that wasn't good enough for Coach Gussler, who knew that I was capable of making that play. He stormed around the fence guarding the dugout screaming, "Get to your feet and throw the damn ball!" I looked around, startled by the yelling. It was funny because I wanted to be mad about being yelled at because I just saved a run, but deep down I knew he was right, and it was at that moment that I knew I had to be better than just good. It was that moment that made me believe in myself.

It's funny to think that a play that was by all accounts a failed play led me to becoming the baseball player I was capable of being. It is also in that moment that I realized that I was just being lazy, trying to show off, and that in this world laziness is seldom rewarded. I quit basketball the following year—funny how things turn out— and focused entirely on baseball after that. I spent every possible moment I could with Coach Gussler, eating up everything he was feeding me.

My focus was rewarded. I finished my final two seasons as a First Team All-OCC selection, First Team All-District (my senior year), earned a scholarship to play for a Division 1 baseball team, made it to the state tournament for

American Legion, and played for Team Ohio. While my parents were always my biggest support, believing in my talents and allowing me to love baseball, I was never really a baseball player until I met Coach Guss, and I attribute much of my baseball success to his tutelage.

After my senior year I returned to Thomas Worthington every winter to practice and lift weights during my college break. It was during this time that I realized just how many lives, besides my own, Coach Gussler had touched. Optional winter workouts turned into must-attend events. Former players would return to work out and practice from all over. Professionals like Eric Crozier and David Cook, college players like myself, Quentin Eberhardt, Mike Dutko, and more were now in attendance.

The number of highly talented athletes that were in attendance only helped to grow the program. Amazingly, a few winter workouts is not where it ended for people who were touched by Coach Gussler. Today, Coach Gussler's staff consists of so many talented former players that are eager to follow and learn more from him, making up the majority of his staff. They often talk about coaching trees at different levels in sports, and Coach Guss' tree is filled with some of the most talented young minds in central Ohio.

Now that I've shared some fun stories about myself and Coach Gussler and how he shaped my life, I want to get serious for a minute about the most amazing part about Coach Gussler. It has to do with his most recent struggles with cancer. It has to do with his incredible ability to constantly show up. It has to do with his commitment to family, friends, and baseball. His competitive nature that doesn't allow him to give up, feel sorry, or back down when others might.

Five years ago now, Coach Gussler was first diagnosed with cancer. When I heard the news, I thought, "There's no way that this could be true." He was so young, strong, and healthy, there must be some mistake. Then I watched him battle surgery and chemo, never missing a beat. Even when he was sick, he still played baseball, pushing those around him to work as hard as he did, while smiling and enjoying the summer sun.

When things got worse and he could no longer play, he still inspired with his matter-of-fact speeches about his condition and scenario, all while remaining positive in the face of often bleak and difficult news. This was the most amazing thing for me. That even when things looked most uncertain, he never let his spirit waver. He never showed anyone around him that he didn't believe he was going to beat this. And that is so rare.

In a world today where few people know what it's like to work hard and sacrifice, Coach Gussler has done more than enough of both for everyone. Even with the pain, difficulty, and various challenges, it would be rare to see him without a smile on his face. Approaching each day with a positive outlook, his battle with cancer has opened many eyes to the amazingly powerful human spirit.

I would be lying if I told you that I wasn't scared about the future. Watching Coach Gussler change from the young, strong, athletic coach that I knew to the weak, skinny, battled man he is today is hard to face. However, his strength gives me strength and hope that if there is anyone who can beat this, it is Coach Gussler.

I recently heard, for the first time in a long time, good news when it comes to the battle Coach Gussler is facing with cancer. Only nine months after being told by the James (a cancer hospital affiliated with Ohio State University) that there were no other options, Coach Gussler had a PET scan that showed only a small spot of cancer. The spot is small enough that they believe they will be able to remove it with a cyberknife in a few weeks, leaving Coach Gussler cancer-free.

Every time I hear someone talk about Coach Gussler, I stop whatever I'm doing to listen. It is because I know that what I'm going to hear is going to make me want to be better, work hard, and believe more. Often when I hear stories of how Coach Gussler has inspired people, it brings me to tears. I'm honored to know such a great man and privileged to have had him change my life. It is because of his strength that I know I will always be stronger as I strive to be GussStrong!

Unfortunately, Coach Guss lost his battle with cancer on May 27, 2014, but the life he led and the lessons he taught still live on today. My pursuit of greatness stems from my time with Coach Guss. I hope he sees my drive and passion for leadership and teaching and smiles down from above. I do my best every day to be present, to love deeply, to smile, and to live each day to the fullest. I hope the lessons and stories in this book inspire you as much as Coach Gussler has inspired me. Give yourself to everything you pursue and live your life GussStrong.

-What is Greatness?-

"Believe that you have a destiny to be great."
-Mark Victor Hansen

It was May 7, 1989, and I was sitting on my living room floor, inches away from my family's old tube television. I was locked in on the NBA game that was unfolding on the screen before me. It had been a back-and-forth game and I could feel the tension rising inside of me. With three seconds left in the game, Craig Ehlo scored to put the Cleveland Cavaliers up by one over the Chicago Bulls and looking like they'd be moving on to the next round of the playoffs. Unfortunately for the Cavs, the Bulls had Michael Jordan.

After the timeout, the Bulls inbounded the ball from just beyond half-court. Jordan was double-teamed but worked to get himself in a position to receive the inbound pass. Upon catching the ball, Jordan took two hard dribbles to his left, put his foot in the ground, and elevated for a jump shot from just behind the free-throw line. He floated in the air for what felt like five seconds as Ehlo floated past him. After a double pump, Jordan released a shot that rattled home as time expired. Jordan ran to the sideline, jumping in the air and pumping his fist over and over. The shot gave the Bulls a 101-100 victory over the Cavs and sent the Bulls into the next round of the playoffs.

Two things happened that day. One, an almost-six-year-old boy's dreams were crushed as his favorite team lost in heartbreaking fashion. So many emotions surged through me as I watched through tear-filled eyes my beloved Cavs walk off the court. And, two, I found myself completely intrigued with greatness and what it took to become great. Jordan in that single moment sparked an interest in me that I still have today. What makes the greats great? Why do some people achieve success where others fail? What sets the successful apart from the average?

As an athlete and sports fan I leaned heavily on studying what great athletes did differently than everyone else. Athletes like Ken Griffey Jr., Mike Tyson, Wayne Gretzky, Michael Johnson, and Jerry Rice became my idols of what is possible if you work hard enough. I was motivated to become the best possible athlete I could and to one day achieve the greatness that these iconic athletes did. More than thirty years later, I am still searching for a deeper and better understanding of what makes the greats great. It's a passion and a search that I don't think will ever end.

I have discovered similarities among all the greats I listed above, but I have also found similarities between the athletes I loved and coaches, leaders, musicians, inventors, and entrepreneurs. Greatness in sports isn't any different from greatness in anything we pursue. The level of commitment to your craft, attention to detail, ability to ignore the critics, and an uncommon level of grit typically shows up in all of these people. It's not that they were born different; they just worked differently. Given the tools all these men utilized, everyone can become great.

I wake up every morning chasing greatness, and I believe I'm on the right path. I've found a calling I'm passionate about. I have committed myself to learning and bettering myself regularly and know that if I continue to do what I'm doing, I will one day achieve success. A really cool thing about my path to greatness is it's tied to other people's greatness and success. My passion for coaching and leading others means that when I finally do reach my greatness, I will have assisted others in achieving their own personal greatness along the way. Knowing this gives me tons of energy and strength.

My hope is that by reading this book you will see that the journey to excellence isn't smooth or easy. The true testament to the excellence of the people referenced in this book is the work they choose to put in—the daily work over years of their lives that eventually allowed them to achieve success. The other thing to remember as you chase your dreams and goals is that there are a lot of things that go into your future success. Don't expect to achieve all your goals tomorrow. Greatness is a war of attrition, and you must stay true to your process through all of the adversity that shows up along the way. Never give up!

"Remember, don't try to build the greatest wall that's ever been built. Focus on laying a single, expertly-placed brick. Then keep doing that, every day." -Will Smith

I'm often asked what my definition of greatness is. What does it mean to be great? I think greatness can be many things. The first thing to understand is that greatness doesn't have to mean being the best at something. It's not about being the best—though as we continue through this book, you'll see that I believe we should all pursue being the best—it's about being *our* best. I want you to pursue being the best, but only one person can claim that title, and greatness is possible without being the best. When I say, "Be great," I'm referring to the journey or pursuit of greatness.

Greatness can look different to different people based on what they're pursuing. Greatness in one pursuit may be very different from greatness in another pursuit. For example, I'm writing this book to deliver a message about greatness not to be seen as a great writer—I don't care about being the best writer—but because I want to be the best coach or teacher. Someone else may want to be remembered as the best writer. We're both producing things via the written word, but our definitions of greatness will be different because mine is based on my message and theirs is based on their writing skills. This can be true in many areas of pursuit, which makes defining greatness difficult. Because greatness can mean different things to different people, I think it's important to focus more on the process of being great.

This book is about the character traits needed in order to discover your personal greatness. Each of our journeys may be different, but the things required of us to become great will be very similar. To discover your full greatness, you must be willing to work, compete, confront failure, embrace adversity, be confident, foster curiosity, live to a higher standard, become self-aware, set goals, and take action daily. Throughout this book I'm going to take you on a journey. It's a journey through past lessons learned and future goals I hope you achieve. Allow me to be your guide on this part of your journey to greatness.

"Excellence is not a destination; it is a continuous journey that never ends." -Brian Tracy

Greatness is a journey. It's a daily pursuit of being better than you were yesterday. It's a battle against yourself and others to improve upon who you are in this moment as you aspire to be more in the next moment. Greatness is a journey of overcoming adversity, facing failure, and dealing with setbacks and triumphs, all while wanting more. Greatness requires honing a myriad of traits and characteristics every day for the entirety of your life. Those who can navigate the uncertain seas of excellence are the ones who one day find themselves in the spotlight of success.

During my time as an athlete, coach, trainer, and podcaster, I've experienced a lot of success and failure. Along the way, I've achieved some high levels of success and I've also fallen short of achieving the ultimate greatness I sought. I want to use this experience to help guide you on the path to excellence. My hope is that some of my failures and shortcomings can teach you where I went wrong so you can avoid the same mistakes.

When I failed to reach success it was no one's fault but my own. I'm human and I lost my way. I went away from what had made me successful and settled for the dangerous "good enough" level of commitment and work. I'm tired of "good enough." I'm over the excuses and permission I've given myself to be anything less than great. We all deserve greatness. Choose a path and commit to it. Jump in with both feet. Don't hold back and give yourself an excuse as to why you might fail.

"Good enough" is a term used by those settling for less than their best. It's used when we get comfortable with where we are. It's used when we don't want to put in the work required to continue to grow. I'm tired of seeing people settle for less than their absolute maximum capabilities. I've watched as I settled for "good enough" and missed a potential opportunity to play professional baseball. I've watched athletes I've worked with settle for "good enough" only to be passed by those who weren't as good as they were a year ago. "Good enough" is settling for average, and we're all capable of so much more than average.

I'm tired of watching people settle for average. I'm tired of watching people make excuses for why they can't do something. I'm tired of the negative comments about someone else's success and the way we diminish people's accomplishments. There is greatness in all of us. No matter who you are, where you're from, or where you start, greatness is available to you if you want it badly enough. The problem isn't your talent or skill; it's your determination and ability to do the work.

So, what really makes someone great? Why do some people rise to the top of their chosen field and others disappear into the crowd of average and ordinary? There are so many stories of people rising to greatness, but just as common is the story of the kid who wasted all their talent. The world is tough on greatness. It challenges those who seek excellence, looking for any weakness it can find, then attacks it with everything it has. I believe this is why we are so enthralled by those who achieve excellence. I also believe that's why we hear so many people claim that these people are great because they're "gifted," "talented," "blessed," or whatever other word is used to make excuses as to why we can't be them.

We are all born with greatness in us. I absolutely believe this to be true. No matter who you are, you have what it takes to become great. We all face limitations to our abilities that may make some tasks harder to achieve than others, but no matter our starting point, greatness is a possible end place. I believe this because greatness is a choice. It's a choice to do more work than those around you. It's a choice to take on adversity and use it as fuel. It's a choice to show up every day with purpose and vision for who you want you become. What choice will you make?

Think about how we're wired for a moment. As children we have all the tools necessary to achieve excellence. Watch a kid explore the world with curiosity and take on challenges with resilience and grit. A kid doesn't fear failure or wonder what the world might think of his failed efforts. A kid doesn't stop to care what someone might say about him as he attempts to accomplish a task that his parents don't believe he can do. We were born with all the traits and tools we need to achieve greatness, but somewhere along the way we divert from our biological code and settle for average and ordinary. I want us to be uncommon and extraordinary.

We need to tap into our childlike fearlessness because the truth about greatness is that failure is going to be part of the journey. You're going to face adversity. You're going to fail and fall short of your goals. You're going to have to change course. There will be people who hate on your journey, and it will be a lot of hard work. The greats don't land at the top: they climb and claw their way there. They invest everything they have into becoming great. They outwork everyone around them. They have purpose and focus on a single goal and pursue it relentlessly until they get a win. Then they turn around, forget the win, and pursue another one. Being great doesn't stop when you find a little success: it continues on the path. At the peak of each mountain, the greats find another, taller mountain to scale.

"A dream does not become reality through magic; it takes sweat, determination, and hard work." -Colin Powell

Since the beginning of recorded human history, we have been inspired and enamored with greatness. It is recognized throughout time. We talk about great civilizations, empires, leaders, artists, musicians, athletes, innovators, and more. This infatuation with greatness has led many to chase success and excellence. We read about greatness in books, we watch movies about it and listen to songs. It has also inspired innovation and athletic achievement. Leaders around the globe seek greatness through their efforts. But what does it really take to become great or achieve greatness?

We love the idea of greatness so much that we name people "Great": Catherine the Great, Alexander the Great, the Great Bambino, The Great One, and "The Greatest." (Muhammad Ali). We also seek out people to label with the moniker "GOAT," or "Greatest Of All Time." This usually leads to heated arguments about whose impact was greater. I find it Interesting that the term used to identify the person who is the best at something involves the word "great" instead of "best" or "excellent."

Some of you may be asking: "What is greatness, and how do we define it?" That's a fair question, and I think if you asked 100 people you'd probably get 100 different answers. In fact, if you Google "greatness," you'll get varying definitions. For me, greatness is a process of daily efforts and consistent habits. There's also an important distinction you must make that you can achieve greatness without being considered the greatest. Too many of us don't see our work as great because someone might be doing better. Let that fuel you, but don't let it belittle your accomplishments.

Like I mentioned above, I believe we all have what it takes to be great and achieve greatness. While I believe we have what it takes, however, I also think most people who seek greatness don't achieve it. It's not because they lack the talent, knowledge, tools, or any other attribute, but because they fail to do all the little things necessary to achieve greatness. While they think they want greatness, they don't commit to the little things that they know are required to pay the toll to greatness.

Greatness is a choice. It's choosing to do the difficult things consistently and pursuing excellence in everything you do. Achieving greatness is difficult. It takes years of dedicated effort to even come close. The path to greatness is simple but not easy, which I think makes it one of the most difficult tasks we take on in life. It would be a lot easier to settle for the comfort of doing average work. It would be easier to stay safe and in your comfort zone while you go through life, but that's not how humans are wired. We're wired to be great, to pursue excellence, to challenge ourselves and make an impact.

As you read through this book, you'll notice that there are no chapter numbers. I stole this from elite personal trainer Tim Grover, who wrote two books using this method. This isn't a list of things to do to be great. There is no "10 Steps to Greatness" list that you can complete and find success. This is a compilation of skills and attributes that the greats share. No one skill or trait is more important than the other. To truly be great, you can't just pick and choose a few to apply and go to work: you must be willing to adopt all of it. Greatness requires a higher standard. If you're not ready to change your standard of excellence, you'll find yourself living an average life filled with great potential.

Now, I'm not trying to take anything away from a person's choice to be average, but I think it's time we acknowledge that average is a choice. We all have the ability to be great. We are all meant for more than average. In order to become great, however, we have to change our standards. We have to demand more of ourselves. We have to commit to doing more work and challenging the status quo every day. It's a difficult way to live and it's not for everyone, but neither is winning. There's a reason why there's only one champion at the end of a season. Be different. Be great!

My goal for this book is to touch on just a couple of the things successful people do. I'm not claiming to have all the answers. The truth about greatness and excellence is that I could write about them for the rest of my life and not cover everything. My goal is to help start you on your path to being great. I want to be your guide on your climb up the mountain you are facing to achieve greatness. We will plan out the best path for you to take and prepare you for the obstacles you are bound to face.

Like I've said a few times now, we all have the ability to be great; sometimes we just need a little help getting started. Once you learn a few of these things, nothing will be able to stop you from achieving your success except you. Throughout this book, I will reference personal experiences and stories as well as conversations I've had with leaders and successful people I've had the privilege to call friends and colleagues. It's time to take on the challenges of pursuing excellence. It's time to stop making excuses. It's time to be great!

I'm writing this book not because I've achieved the ultimate level of greatness—I'm still working on that. I'm writing this because through my years as an athlete, coach, mentor, trainer, and podcaster, I've been exposed to many extremely great people. I've experienced wins and losses, successes and failures, and I'm trying to help you navigate the ones you're bound to face on your way to the top. Greatness doesn't come easy. While others have written stories about success and how to get there, I know, as any great coach knows, the more voices we can get saying the same things, the greater the chance of our message hitting home. I hope this book inspires you to make some changes in your life and to begin to chase greatness. Reach for the stars. You may fall flat on your face, but remember, whenever you fall, always get up.

"Greatness is a lot of small things done well. Day after day, workout after workout, obedience after obedience, day after day." -Ray Lewis

-Work Is the Way-

"Talent is cheaper than table salt. What separates the talented individual from the successful one is hard work." -Stephen King

Too many people today are looking for the easy way. The shortcut to success. The ten steps to a better you. The higher-paying job without having ever done the work to get there. This entitlement and expectation of more without doing work hinders our ability to become our greatest self. Too many people think they can just start at the top, but the truth is, you can't escape the work. The hard reality is there is no easy way to success.

Success isn't complicated. In fact, it's simple. But simple and easy are two very different things. We know the path to greatness. The truth about becoming great has been laid out so many different times by now that it's not some surprising or earth-shattering revelation I'm sharing. Get up early, work hard for hours every day, learn from your mistakes, repeat. Obviously, there are some nuances in this plan for each path to greatness, but the building blocks are fairly well-known. So, while there are many ways to the top, all of them require putting in work. If you're looking for easy then you're not looking for success. Work is the way.

By this point in my career I've read a number of books on success and greatness, as well as been around some very successful people, and if there is one thing that consistently stands out about them, it's this: They love the work. They look forward to practice. They look forward to getting down in the dirt and pushing themselves to new levels. They crave being uncomfortable and the hours that it takes to master a skill. Successful people look for ways to get more work in than everyone else. They don't look for shortcuts or ways around the work; they try to find time to put in more work.

Kobe Bryant is a perfect example of this. His work ethic and drive were unmatched. He was getting a sweat and putting up shots hours before anyone else was even waking up. When most people were going to their first workout of the day, he was finishing up his second. Even after making it to the peak of his sport, this was his way. There was no replacement for the time he put into his craft. This mindset and drive lasted beyond his playing days, and I really wish we could have seen just how great he would have been after basketball.

On the other end of the spectrum is the progression of my baseball career. I've always been a hard worker, or so I believe. I was a first-to-practice, last-to-leave kid all through high school. I spent extra hours hitting and in the weight room. I was focused on putting in work. I loved the work. I spent hours doing work while my friends were going to parties, hanging out on Friday nights at the football games, and being kids. This work gave me a chance to play Division 1 baseball.

There was a moment during my high school career that I believe is relevant here. I was playing shortstop and there was a hard ground ball to my right. I took two hard steps and dove into the hole. I fielded the ball cleanly, but as I attempted to transfer the ball and make the throw from my knees, I dropped the ball and the runner was safe. The play kept the runner on second from scoring, but no outs were recorded.

As I sat there on my knees, disappointed I didn't get an ESPN Top Ten play, my coach, Stephen Gussler, came flying around the fence of our dugout screaming, "Get to your feet and throw the damn ball!"

I was confused. Was he yelling at me? I had just made a diving play. What could he be yelling at me for? In the moment, I was angry that he would yell at me after a play like that, but after the game we talked and he explained what he was upset about.

He looked at me and said, "You're a special player, and that play was extremely difficult. I didn't yell because you didn't get the out; I yelled because you took the easy way out. You tried to take the shortcut by throwing from your knees instead of continuing to work hard to get to your feet and make a strong throw. There are no shortcuts to greatness. You have to keep working hard even after the initial hard work is done. Don't just do part of the work—do it all."

I've never forgotten this moment, and it's one that I'll pass on to everyone I get the chance to coach. That was a moment that changed a lot for me, and I told myself that I wouldn't be outworked by anyone as long as I played.

I stayed true to this work ethic my first year at Youngstown State University. I spent extra hours hitting, lifting, and doing anything I could to set myself apart from the crowd. I earned a starting spot my freshman year and became a Louisville Slugger First Team Freshman All-American. I was paving a path toward the professional career I wanted.

But then I got comfortable. I skipped the extra batting sessions, I finished up my lifts with the rest of my team, I went out on the weekends, and I wasn't the first to practice or the last to leave. I got comfortable with my success, and because I got comfortable, my success left me.

I didn't stop working, but I didn't keep the level of discipline and hard work that earned me success to begin with. I still had a solid career at Youngstown State, but I did not have the career I believe I was capable of, and it was for no other reason than my loss of focus on putting in the work. It's hard to look back now and own up to those shortcomings, but my hope is that my loss of focus and effort will be an eye-opener to everyone that success is short-term. The work never stops. The time at the top of any mountain is short-lived, and if you get too comfortable there, someone will pass you by. Work harder than everyone else, enjoy the success that comes with it—but only for a moment—then get back to work.

The most difficult part about work is there isn't an instant return on investment, so once you start to have a little success, you don't feel like the additional hours are necessary anymore. The other part of the equation is you don't lose the success you've acquired by skipping the extra work. It's only over time that the results start to wane and the competition begins to catch up. By then it's too late. You no longer have that lead you had built with the hours of extra work: you have to start again from the bottom. Don't get lost in moments of success, especially when they're not your final destination.

"A dream does not become reality through magic; it takes sweat, determination, and hard work." -Colin Powell

I was always a hard worker as an athlete. Even before middle school, I was all about the hard work. I started a training program with a friend of mine to improve my vertical jump when I was twelve years old. Every day I would get with my friend Nick Switzer and jump until my legs burned, but the work never bothered me. I was always married to the work. I knew that, no matter what happened, I didn't want to go into a competition and fear that the person I was facing had outworked me. Every day and everything I did was go hard or go home. If I was going to do work, I was going to work hard.

As my career in sports as a player ended and I became more involved as a coach, I watched the kids around me closely. Over the last decade, I've helped more than a hundred kids achieve the dream of playing in college. I have kids who have played every sport you can imagine: golf, swimming, tennis, basketball, baseball, football, volleyball, softball, and soccer. Each kid and sport were vastly different, but most of my kids who make it as college athletes have one very important thing in common: They work hard.

My most successful kids weren't just pure athletes, though I've had a few of those. My best athletes were my hardest workers. They were the kids who would ask to stay after practice and do extra work. They were the kids who would show up early and work out on their own. They were the kids who pushed their teammates to work harder and never cut corners. The hard work was part of their drive to be great. I had kids who would come in to work out at 6 a.m. during the season because it was the only time they had available and they wouldn't miss a workout.

As I've mentioned a few times now, there are no shortcuts, and the best athletes I've worked with have embraced this truth. They choose to be the hardest workers in the room. Some of them were hard workers before they got to me and just needed their work aimed in the right direction. Some of them weren't hard workers, however. Some just believed they were athletic and that was enough. At the end of the day, though, success doesn't really show up until you decide you're going to work for it.

One of my favorite stories of this is about a young man I coached in baseball at Pickerington Central (a school in a suburb southeast of Columbus, Ohio). AJ came into the program extremely talented. He had natural gifts that made him a special player, but he was also friends with some of the most talented kids in the school. I think this was something that hurt him early in his career, as he saw their success and acted as if he should have that as well. I loved AJ. He was a great kid who I knew could be special, but he didn't have the work ethic to match his gifts.

Over the course of his high school career he struggled to consistently play for the varsity team. He bounced up and down between JV and varsity and often found himself in trouble. I continued to invest in him, and I always believed in him. We had some incredible conversations about how he was sabotaging himself and his future. Then something clicked, and I saw a shift during his senior year. He began to work more, work harder, and dig deeper into the details of success. He became a leader, and I'm not sure I ever saw a kid work harder. AJ became a different athlete with a renewed energy.

AJ's senior year was something special. AJ became one of the most dominant hitters in the state of Ohio while leading his team to a conference championship and a district final. AJ also earned First Team All-OCC (conference recognition) and All-District honors while becoming a First Team All-Ohio selection. This kid who struggled to be an everyday player was now being recognized as one of the best players in the state. What changed? How does a kid go from a player who bounced around between JV and varsity to such an incredible leader and player?

The only real change for AJ was his focus on the work. He committed himself to the weight room, hitting extra, learning the game, and developing his mental game. He had weekly meetings with the head coach to develop a better relationship and learn more about the game. AJ didn't all of a sudden grow into a different person physically. In fact, he was pretty banged up for most of his senior year. His gifts didn't change overnight from a weak young athlete to a man —he was a man among boys for most of his career. The biggest change was his intentional focus on doing work, and the results speak for themselves.

"I've always believed that if you put in the work, the results will come. I don't do things half-heartedly.

Because I know if I do, then I can expect half-hearted results." -Michael Jordan

I believe the reason we think greatness is out of our reach most of the time is because we are constantly seeing the finished product. Every time we watch a professional athlete perform, an actor in a movie, a singer on stage at the Grammys, or watch a brilliant educator give a TED Talk, we're seeing a finished product. We're seeing the culmination of days, weeks, months, and years of hard work in a singular moment. What we don't see is the time and effort it took for that person to get to that level of success and proficiency. Of course we're going to see this and think we can't possibly do that. But if we take a moment to think about how much work that person did to achieve that level of excellence, we can then begin to decide whether we have the strength to put in the work to reach that level.

In today's world we get to see a small glimpse of this work through behind-the-scenes videos on social media or some "30 for 30" on ESPN, but even that is just a glimpse, a fraction of the actual work that goes into making these people the best at what they do. There's no shortcut available to avoid the work. We need to stop making excuses as to why we can't be these people we see on the big stage and understand that we all have the ability to be great. We just need to up our standard of excellence. We need to dig in and do the work.

I think there's a part of human nature that makes us put excellence on a pedestal. We put people who achieve greatness in a separate category from "normal" people. We treat them as if they have some superpower or special gift that allowed them to succeed. By telling ourselves that they're just special, it gives us an out as to why we're not where they are. It's a defense mechanism to guard against potential failure. It's the easy way out for us to avoid the hard work needed to achieve excellence.

Imagine if you decided to dedicate yourself to becoming the best at something. You have committed to putting in the work. As a part of your attempt to improve, you decide that for each practice that everyone else is doing, you will show up fifteen minutes early and stay fifteen minutes late each day. If you have practice five days a week, you're getting an additional two and a half hours of practice each week. Let's draw this out for the month, year, five years, and ten years: that's ten extra hours each month, 130 hours each year, 650 hours over five years, and 1,300 hours over ten years.

That's the compound power of committing to doing just a little bit more work than required. Each year you get five and a half more days (let that sink in: days!) of work than everyone else on your team. When you reach the ten-year mark, you've put in more than 54 additional days of work—almost two extra months. How much better do you think you'd be compared to your competition, having worked on something for an additional 1,300 hours? Imagine how much more you'll accomplish in the next ten years.

This is what sets the best apart from everyone else. It's not some innate ability or secret talent. It's the compound effort of more work. Again, we're only seeing the finished product, not the countless hours and days that went into who they are now. The best are always looking for an advantage, and they find it in doing more than everyone else around them. The best students study more, the best athletes train more, the best actors rehearse more, the best inventors tinker more, the best musicians play more. The common denominator is they do more.

"I start early and I stay late, day after day after day, year after year. It took me 17 years and 114 days to become an overnight success." -Lionel Messi

As I sit here writing this, the 2020 Tokyo Olympics are going on. I find myself listening to announcers claim time and time again that these athletes are special, gifted, talented, one of a kind. While I agree they're special, it's not because of something they were born with or given; it was something they earned. When announcers or broadcasters say they're talented, they're sending the message to those watching that you probably shouldn't even try because you're not that gifted. Which is total bullshit. Anyone reading this has what it takes to be great. The other thing they're doing is discrediting the effort and work that these incredible athletes have put in over the last couple of decades just to have a chance to compete at this moment.

Now, I'd be remiss to completely ignore certain facts about talent and gifts if I didn't mention a few things here. Everyone is born with particular gifts, and it's up to you to discover what those are and how best to use them. We are all born with strengths and weaknesses. Understanding how to use those strengths and weaknesses can give you an advantage on your quest for greatness. You can outwork your weaknesses if you honestly address them, or you can lean into your strengths and work them to become stronger. Either way, owning the work is paramount to future success.

Sure, it helps to be six-foot-eight if you want to play in the NBA. It helps to have long limbs and a short torso if you want to be a swimmer. It's beneficial to be compact and smaller as a gymnast. It helps to have a naturally controlled vocal range to be a singer.

But I think this is also part of the problem. We only look at particular ways to use our gifts. Gifts and talents help, but without developing those talents, we don't accomplish anything. I've seen many tall people who can't play basketball. I've seen many short people who can't do a flip or balance on a beam. It really comes down to developing our talents into strengths that allow us to be great and excel.

Usain Bolt is one of my favorite athletes. He's arguably the best sprinter of all time and will be at the top of that conversation for years to come. His six-foot-five frame and powerful long strides give him a unique advantage for max speed, but there are plenty of six-foot-five athletes who aren't as fast as him. What makes him special is that he spent years developing his speed to become the elite sprinter we know him as today.

I recently read that Usain Bolt spent a total of 114 seconds on the track during Olympic finals, during which he won six Olympic gold medals over three Olympic games. So from 2008 to 2016 he raced in final events for less than two minutes and we're going to tell people it's because he's gifted or talented. There's no way he didn't consistently put in work over that time to prepare for each of these meets. I use this example to show you the product you see in the big moments is just a fraction of the work that is done to be able to compete there. There's no way around the work; there's only the work. So figure out what you want to be great at and go to work!

It's time as a community seeking greatness that we embrace the work we all need to do to achieve our excellence. It will not be handed to us. It will not show up one day on our doorstep, gift-wrapped with a bow on it. The truth is, even if greatness were that easy, people who find it this way never keep it. This is why we see so many young people achieve high levels of success only to disappear into the world and be forgotten. Without the trials and tribulations and the understanding of the work it takes to reach the top, we don't know what it takes to stay there when we arrive. If you're out there praying to achieve greatness or get success without embracing the work that goes with it, you will never have what it takes to keep it. This is why the work is so important. The difficulty that comes from getting our hands dirty and getting to work teaches us the discipline we need to have long-term success.

A friend of mine told me a story about a person who was looking to get in shape by doing hikes with the least amount of walking possible. Let that sink in for a moment. How do you plan on achieving a better level of conditioning and health without working for it? I mean, the word "work" is in "workout"! You can't exercise without work. When I heard this, it just solidified my belief that we've become too comfortable with things. Too many people today want things without earning them. We want money without working for it. We want education without paying for it. We want, we want, we want. The truth is, you can want a lot of things, but most of them don't come without some work.

The other piece of this is we don't value things we get for free. There's no appreciation for stuff that's handed to us. It's like running unopposed. You didn't win anything. Without hard work, the result carries little weight. I want you to think about something you've won that didn't take a lot of effort. Now, think about something that took everything you had to give to achieve. Assuming you could even think of something for the first part, I guarantee the second memory is more impactful. We remember the hard times and the good that comes from working through them. Nobody cares about the stuff that we didn't work for; it doesn't mean anything.

I have a friend who's currently working on his first novel. By the time this book is finished I'm hoping that he has earned a book deal. He's been writing this book for more than five years. This is his second attempt to publish the book after doing a complete rewrite. When he finally gets his deal, it's going to mean so much to him. He's going to be so excited and proud, as will I, and it's because of all the hard work that it is going to happen. If he would have written the book, submitted one query letter and got signed, he'd be happy, but it wouldn't mean as much.

At the end of the day we want to work hard. It's in our nature as human beings to work hard. Since we were a society of hunters and gatherers, the hardest workers were the ones to survive, and that is still with us. The key is to find something you're willing to work for. Obviously, we're past the point of working to survive, so it's up to us to decide where we aim that effort. We all have what it takes to do the work.

So find something you want and roll up your sleeves and get after it. There are no shortcuts. There is no "easy button." Stop looking for a way to avoid the work and lean into the difficulty that is bound to accompany your goals of greatness. Trust the process and in the end you'll appreciate your success more and know better how to keep it once you've found it. The work is the way! Dream big, and dream about all the work it's going to take to get there. Each day you spend working toward your dreams is a day well spent. Nobody is going to hand you your dreams—it's time to go to work!

Action Steps:

If you're really looking to start your journey toward greatness, it starts with accepting the work. There's no way around it. In order to see the results you want, the first thing you have to do is accept that your dreams aren't going to be accomplished tomorrow. There are no shortcuts. As you continue to read through this book and set your mind on the thing you want to truly be great at, remember that it starts with picking something you're willing to show up for.

As you set your sights, ask yourself these questions:

- How much am I willing to work to make this dream my reality?
- Do I love working toward this goal?
- Am I willing to give up things I like to do for the things I have to do?
- Will I outwork everyone else?
- Am I willing to show up early or stay late?
- Will I work every day without knowing when the work might be done?

Remember, every dream you have is possible if you're willing to put in the work. Everything you want in this life starts with the work. Pick a dream that you know you will wake up each day and devote yourself to. Choose something you can see yourself working on for years without losing energy or passion. It may take a lot of effort to find this dream, but once you do, greatness is within your reach. Go be great!

"The elevator to success is out of order. You'll have to use the stairs…one step at a time." -Joe Girard

-Motivation is Bullshit: Passion, Purpose, and Discipline are King-

"If you spend too much time thinking about a thing, you'll never get it done. Make at least one definitive move daily toward your goal."
-Bruce Lee

When we think of motivation, what we're usually thinking of is enthusiasm or inspiration: what we experience when we're really excited to do something and it's coming easily to us. Enthusiasm and inspiration are only two types of motivation, however, and they can't be your sole source of fuel when trying to achieve greatness. They're unreliable, and they often won't be there when you want them or need them. You need to put more stock into deeper, steadier forms of motivation, like discipline, passion, purpose, and commitment.

As you can see, there are many forms of motivation, and using these appropriately can create enormous possibilities. I'm going to use this chapter to tell you a story and paint a picture about how we can use the many forms of motivation to navigate the seas of possibility. Along the journey to greatness you will encounter many different forms of motivation. You will have moments when you'll feel inspired and enthusiastic about the work. You will have moments when you must lean into the discipline of doing the little things every day. There will be days when you must rely on your commitment and dedication to getting to your goals. Sometimes you'll also find that you must shift slightly in a new direction or change course entirely.

I believe we're all floating along in an ocean of possibilities. We have endless directions we can go. Sometimes we see land on the horizon, and other times it feels as if we're searching for any sign that we're not alone on this journey. Ultimately, it is up to us to pick a direction and get the boat moving. As we navigate this vast ocean, we must use everything we have at our disposal to reach our destination. We must build a strong boat, set our sails, harness the wind, row when necessary, check our heading, and adjust our setting when we roam off course. If we rely too heavily on one thing, the journey becomes longer and we may never reach our final destination. Let's navigate these seas and harness the many powers of motivation.

"Don't expect to be motivated every day to get out there and make things happen. You won't be. Don't count on motivation. Count on discipline." -Jocko Willlink

Like the chapter title states, motivation is bullshit. However, I think it's important to expand upon this to say that if we rely solely on one type of motivation, that is the bullshit. More than anything, I think that believing you will feel enthusiastic and inspired every day sets you up for a long and tedious journey, one that will constantly be reliant on which way the winds are blowing on a particular day. As we look to navigate the seas of possibility, using the power of the wind is important. It's the most powerful source of energy we have available to propel our boat in the direction we want to go. It's also the most unreliable, however.

We never really know when the wind is going to blow. We don't know which direction it's going to blow or when it's going to leave us floating along without any assistance. Relying on the wind to get us to our destination is going to create a lot of obstacles to overcome. When it does show up, however, we have to be ready to harness its power. We can't miss an opportunity to use the wind to propel us forward quickly and to gain some significant momentum toward our destination.

As you can see, relying on the wind to take us where we want to go isn't going to cut it. This is where discipline, commitment, passion, and purpose come into play. Discipline is doing the little things every day to help us reach our destination. It's checking that the boat is in good working order—looking for leaks, checking the heading, preparing the sails, and setting the sails—even if the wind isn't blowing. The discipline is important because if the boat isn't ready for when the wind does blow, you'll miss an opportunity to make positive strides toward achieving your goals.

When I think about discipline, I think about my exercise habits. I've been working out since I was in sixth grade. You would think motivation (enthusiasm and inspiration) wouldn't be a problem for me, but even today while writing this chapter I battled motivation to get my workout in. All the way up to the point where I started my warmup, I kept telling myself I could just skip today's workout and make it up later.

It wasn't my motivation, in the sense of being excited, that got me through my workout—it was my discipline and standards that forced me into action. Then a funny thing happened: As I got started, I found myself starting to get into my workout more and feel good about what I was doing. I felt a surge of enthusiasm and inspiration to work harder and keep building upon the work I was putting in. In the end, I completed a solid, strong workout despite having no enthusiasm when I started.

When we tie this back into our "ocean of possibilities" idea, this was me putting my sails up even though there wasn't any wind, then deciding to start to row the boat. As the boat began to move and we were making progress, a surge of wind came. Luckily, I didn't wait for the wind or I might have missed it. Instead, I stayed true to my commitment and set the sail. Now I am enjoying the strong push of a gust of inspiration.

To be honest, working out now is harder for me than it was years ago. Part of that is because when I first started working out, I was doing it because I knew I needed to be strong and athletic if I was going to be a professional athlete. I was willing to suffer through difficult training sessions because my desire to be great fueled me to push through the lapses in motivation. Exercising was part of my purpose. Nowadays I work out without a particular goal in mind, and this makes daily pursuits of exercise significantly more challenging. I have to lean heavily on my discipline.

Too often we wait to feel motivated to start something. We just sit there waiting for the wind to blow. I think this stems from when we are young. When we're young, we are very highly motivated to do and try new things. We're also easily distracted and don't notice the lulls between gusts. Unfortunately, the older we get and the longer we do things, the less our motivation is available to help us. The newness eventually wears off and the grind of doing anything great sets in. In these moments, we must rely on action to get us through. Our action creates momentum, which leads to motivation. It's interesting, really, if you think about it.

Take a moment now to think about a time you had a dream or goal that wasn't achievable without long-term, consistent effort. Have you ever wanted to write a book, run a marathon, get in the best shape of your life, start a business, become a professional athlete? All of these things take time to achieve, and just like becoming great, the time component eventually wears away the motivation. Sure, day one you're motivated. You're amped up and raring to go.

You hit the ground running, feeling great. What about a month later, six months, a year, five years? Are you still amped up and raring to go? Odds are, not every day. Probably more days than not, you dread the work that has to be done to achieve your dream.

Like I mentioned before, I've been lifting weights since I was in sixth grade. Since that time, I've had only a handful of moments where I haven't lifted at least once during a week. That's 1,352 continuous weeks of training. Now, there were some active recovery weeks following a long season and some vacation workouts that were done via hiking and non-traditional weight-lifting, but I've been consistently active a minimum of three days a week for the last 26 years. That means I've completed more than 4,500 workouts. I'd say I've been excited about my workouts, at most, 50 percent of those times. Most of those were earlier in my training life. That means for more than 2,000 workouts I had to rely on something other than enthusiasm to complete my workout.

I don't tell you these numbers to boast about my fitness performance, but to share that when you do anything for an extended period of time you can't rely solely on excitement and inspiration. Eventually, that is going to fade. Eventually, you're going to have to find another fuel to keep you going. The longer you stick with something, the harder that thing becomes. This is because daily grind takes its toll, plus the newness wears off and you know what is expected of you. And if you're on a path to greatness, you know that it's about to be hard. Nobody wants to do hard work all the time, but the greats find a way to do the hard work even when they don't want to. They have the discipline to set the sails, whether they have the wind or not.

"It is action that creates motivation." -Steve Backley

The next part of our motivation journey is commitment. Commitment is the oars we can use to keep our boat moving no matter what weather we're facing. We have the ability to get the boat where we want it to go without the wind or our sails if we're truly committed to making it. If we're committed to making it happen, nobody can stop us from rowing the boat. Something to remember, though, is that it takes discipline to put the oars in the water each day and go to work. The combination of discipline and commitment can become an extremely powerful tool, and one we must learn to yield effectively to see long-term success.

Commitment is what keeps people coming back to the gym following their New Year's resolutions after the first few months. I still remember how every year my gym staff and I would have this wave of new people at the beginning of the year, all inspired and excited to start on their fitness goals. Then by March, 85 percent of them are nowhere to be found. The enthusiasm wears off and those who aren't truly committed to making a change are gone.

We can commit ourselves to something before the discipline of doing it takes over. You must first commit to doing the thing you want to do, then, over time, your consistent work becomes a discipline. My exercise habits started with a commitment to putting in work to become the best athlete I could, and now the discipline of that habit allows me to continue to exercise even though my athletic career is long over.

Tap into the power of commitment and create the habits necessary to excel over time. Excitement, enthusiasm, and inspiration are not sustainable for success. True success is about doing what needs to be done no matter how you feel that day. If we are always waiting to be moved to do something, nothing will get done. Commit yourself to doing the work, have the discipline to do the work no matter how you feel, and the rest will fall into place.

Another thing I think the common fitness center member fails to do is understand their purpose or "Why" for going to the gym. I don't think they're any less motivated to get in shape than an elite athlete, bodybuilder, or fitness professional. They still want to get in shape, they still want to feel better and look better, but that motivation to be healthy isn't enough to push them to action. The desire for something has to be great enough to endure the work that is required to get it.

The person who wants to be a great author must write for years, constantly editing and fine-tuning his skills. The athlete must practice skills and train their body to be in peak physical condition. A musician will spend hours upon hours playing the same notes over and over so they can get a better feel for the chords. Anyone who has achieved expert-level skill has done so through a deeper purpose and constant practice and work. They took time to look deeper. Otherwise, that motivation fades and becomes just a wish or a want. Unfortunately, over time, the excitement and enthusiasm doesn't last, and when it fades, what do you lean on to create action?

A good way to help create action is to know where you want that action to go. This is your purpose. Your purpose is the compass on your boat. It points you in the right direction and allows you to make adjustments along the way to make sure you stay on course. Without knowing where you want to go, a lot of the other forms of motivation don't really matter. The "greats" have a clear picture of where they're going. They see it in vivid detail and know exactly what it's going to look like once they arrive. Find your purpose and use it as a compass to guide your boat where you want it to go. That way you're always using the wind and rowing the boat in the right direction.

I think this is why it's important to dig deeper into our desires and goals. What's the underlying reason for your motivation to achieve something? What is your Why? What is your purpose? What is your passion? I think having a strong understanding of these three questions provides you the additional direction needed to outlast your enthusiasm and continue to take action toward your goals. Fully embracing these deeper questions can act as the spark necessary to light the fuse on our motivation.

Right now, as I write this book between clients and after my kids go to sleep every night, I feel motivated to put words to paper through a deeper understanding of my "Why," purpose, and passion. I believe writing this book to be a part of my calling. I'm looking to impact the world to fulfill my "Why," and this book can be a tool to allow me to have a greater reach. My Why in this life is to help others.

Through everything I do, the root of it all is to serve those I love in an attempt to make them better. I train to help people achieve better health and fitness. I coach to help people realize their full potential. I show up when asked and help in any way I can. Everything I pursue in my life revolves around this Why. When I choose to do something, I ask, "Does this help someone?" or, "How can doing this help someone?"

I believe I was led to my Why through those who have impacted my life so deeply. I had great parents who supported me in every way. I had an incredible high school coach who pushed and motivated me. I've had incredible friends who believed in me and helped me to be more. I don't fully know how I came to this purpose, but I know when I'm helping others I feel alive and inspired to do more. I also know that when I wake up each day, I'm excited about the possibility of helping someone do more today.

Finding and understanding my Why has led me to my purpose, which is to be a coach in all facets of my life. I believe I was put here to be a coach. I was created to be able to help inspire others, to listen and assist in the development of those around me, and to provide support for others' success. Through others' success I, too, will find growth and success. I'm excited daily knowing that I'm going to have at least one conversation with someone in a coaching setting. This purpose fuels my passion.

Passion is an important part of pursuing something hard. When you find that you're passionate about something, you have to nurture that passion and help it grow. When we're thinking about our boat sailing through the ocean of possibilities, our passion is the current direction we're going. It is controlled by the rudder of our boat. We can change course easily and adjust for new passions and changes in our current direction. It's important, though, not to change direction too often and get lost following passions that don't serve our purpose.

Right now my passions are writing this book, working on my podcast, and developing my knowledge to be a better leader and coach. Each of these things I pursue stems from a deeper understanding of my Why and purpose. How does writing this book help my Why and purpose? Hopefully, it has a message in it that you can become great. Maybe it inspires you to pursue your Why more or gives you information to help you on your personal journey to excellence. It gives me a greater chance to help others. The podcast is the same way as it puts me in front of experts and allows me to share knowledge they have about achieving success. This sharing of knowledge hopefully helps my listeners. The more knowledgeable I become and the better a leader I am, the stronger my skills are to help those who need it. Everything I'm doing stems from a Why that is centered around helping others.

This deeper understanding provides the additional boost to push through days where motivation is lacking. It gives us the ability to hold course through a storm or row when the winds die down. Because no matter how excited we are about something at the beginning, eventually we will need more than motivation and excitement to stick to it. Eventually, the work required will become more difficult, and in those moments we have to stay committed, lean into passion, lean into purpose, and trust in your Why.

"If you have a strong purpose in life, you don't have to be pushed. Your passion will drive you there." -Roy T. Bennett

In the previous section I talked about purpose and passion and how they help you direct your boat where you want it to go. Finding and understanding these two things can be vital to the success you seek. There have been times in my life where I lost sight of my purpose and therefore my passion either became misplaced or lost altogether.

One of these times happened during my freshman year of high school. This situation was actually not a lack of purpose—I knew I wanted to be a college athlete—but a misunderstanding of my passion. I understood where I wanted to go—that was very clear—but I didn't know how to steer my boat to give me the best opportunity to get there.

I had just finished my freshman basketball season and was excited about the upcoming travel season. I had had a very good season, and my team was set to be extremely competitive through the spring and summer. However, I was also about to start school baseball. I felt I was able to do both, but my high school coach was completely against it, saying that it was baseball season and I needed to commit myself to baseball now. I could play basketball later.

I didn't like this, so I went home telling my parents I wanted to quit baseball and focus on my basketball career. I spilled all the reasons I wanted to quit and told them how unfair my coach was being by not letting me do both baseball and basketball. My mom listened to my complaints and took in everything I said. She then said that if I was going to quit, I would first have to talk to three people who were removed from the situation. If I still wanted to quit after that, then I could.

I agreed to these terms as my mother tried to figure out who she was going to ask to talk to me. She knew that me quitting baseball would be a mistake. She also knew I'd only resist more if she told me that instead of letting me figure it out on my own. Luckily for me, my mother knew exactly how to get through to me. She reached out to my middle school athletic director, Bill Mosca. I had built a good relationship with Mr. Mosca during my time at Worthingway Middle School (in Worthington, Ohio), and she hoped he could make sense of things for me.

We went to talk with Mr. Mosca, and he didn't waste any time getting into the meat of my situation. He looked at me and asked, "What is it that you want to do?"

"I want to play Division 1 sports," I replied.

He nodded. "OK, so if you had the chance to play Division 3 basketball or Division 1 baseball, which would you choose?"

I didn't hesitate. "Division 1 baseball."

"And what if you took that off the table?" Mr. Mosca questioned.

I felt my brain go to work and began to calculate what he'd just said. He knew I was a good athlete. He had seen me play basketball at Worthingway for the past two years, during which time our team had one loss and two championships. He also knew that I was five-foot-eleven and not the ideal basketball recruit. Lastly, he understood that I had an opportunity to be a very good baseball player. Based on my size and skill and the fact that I was a freshman playing up (making the junior varsity team), chances were I was going to become much better at baseball than basketball.

I don't remember much more about that conversation, but I do know my mom didn't have to find two more people for me to talk to. I returned to baseball the next day and never looked back. Within a week of practice starting, I was called up to the varsity team and never missed a start during my four years at Thomas Worthington. The funny part is, I eventually quit basketball to focus on my baseball career and became a Division 1 baseball player.

This situation reminds me that while I knew clearly what my purpose was at this time in my life—I wanted to be a Division 1 athlete—I was steering the boat in the wrong direction and following a momentary passion that wasn't in line with my larger purpose. I was following a love of a game that I wasn't best suited to pursue. Now, I'm not saying I couldn't have made a career out of basketball had I committed myself to that game during this time, but I do think that, had I decided in that moment without clearly thinking through the decision, it would have been the wrong one.

We must feel out our passion and follow it when it serves our larger purpose. We must also be willing to step back and check our heading to make sure that the passion we're following gives us the best chance to achieve our purpose. If we don't step back and survey the situation we're in, we find ourselves too close to everything and don't even realize we're pointed in the wrong direction until it's too late. Allow yourself the chance to step back and view the full picture. You might need to adjust your oars a little in order to fulfill your purpose.

"To succeed you have to believe in something with such a passion that it becomes a reality." -Anita Roddick

I want to share a story with you that strays from our journey through the ocean of possibilities for a moment. This is a story about passion. It's about using passion to fuel your internal fire. We will all have sparks of enthusiasm and inspiration throughout our life, but what we do with that spark is critical to who we become. Will you do what it takes to make sure your passion works for you instead of allowing yourself to blindly follow the next passing fancy that pops up? As I mentioned above, using your purpose to decide whether to follow your passion is a great place to start.

Passion is a hot-button topic. It is brought up all the time. Kids and adults are often heard saying, "I'm following my passion" or being told, "Follow your passion." I wonder, however: Is this the right message? Is it our passion that we should follow? How do we decide whether a particular passion is the one we should follow? Do we just blindly bounce from one passion to another?

I believe passion is valuable. I also believe that finding a passion for the work you do and the life you're living is crucial to feeling fulfilled. I often wonder, though, if we know what we're getting into when we follow our passion without knowing what that really means.

Let me start by saying that I am very fulfilled in the work I do. I'm passionate about helping people become better versions of themselves. The means by which I implement this passion has evolved, however. I started as a trainer, using physical fitness to help people better themselves. I transitioned to working as a high school coach and helping our young people learn lessons on life, work, sports, and more. Today, I'm a little bit of many things, but the focus is still on coaching and helping people. I work with athletes, I coach, I mentor, I have a podcast, I engage in meaningful conversations and constantly try to learn and think deeply about who I am, but all of this aligns with my passion for helping others.

I do believe you should find a passion you want to commit your life to. I don't think you should just follow your passion blindly, however. I think you have to find a passion you're willing to nurture and grow.

You have to be aware of who you are and whether that passion fits your situation.

Passion is a spark. But the point of a spark is to create a fire. A spark without the right fuel dies. In your current situation, do you have the resources to turn your spark into a fire? Is there enough kindling to create a flame, enough sticks to fuel a fire, and enough logs to sustain it over time? Passion may ignite a spark, but without these other things, that's all it will ever be. As I mentioned above, if you're passionate about something that doesn't fit your life or environment, it's like building a fire with wet wood. It's going to be very hard to ignite that fire.

You need to be sure your passion has enough wood, oxygen, and space to grow and flourish. If you neglect your fire, it will eventually burn out. This is another part of the analogy that is critical: You may be able to get a fire started, but what are you willing to do to keep that fire burning? Will you protect it from the elements? Will you keep it burning in a controlled environment or just let it run ablaze, destroying everything around you? Finding a passion is great, but keeping a passion alive takes time and effort.

Once you find something you think you're passionate about, you have to determine whether this is a true passion or a momentary infatuation. Ask yourself if you are willing to sacrifice to keep this fire burning. Do you have the discipline required to keep your fire burning? Will you get up in the middle of the night to feed the fire if it gets low? Will you hold an umbrella over it when it rains? Will you build a cover to keep it burning for an extended period of time? Being passionate about something is great, but what will you do to continue to develop that passion?

Ultimately, if you've found a passion that is true, you'll find you're willing to do anything to keep your fire burning. Once you find that thing you're willing to work at to build and grow and keep adding sticks to the flame, the tasks required to nurture it no longer feel like sacrifices. You're not sacrificing to keep it going, you're doing what is required to build your passion into a bonfire. You're putting in the time and effort to keep adding logs to the fire. You begin to think of the things you do as a choice to fan the flames of your passion, not as a sacrifice to build a fire.

I believe as you continue to strive to be great you need to take time to contemplate your passion. I hope you choose to reflect on the questions I asked above. I believe that blindly following a passion is a potential recipe for disaster. Be cautious with how you use the sparks that show up in your life. Be cautious about abandoning an old fire for something new: the environment may not be as conducive to building a flame as where you're at now.

As you continue to move through this life, I hope you find passion in the things you do. I hope you find joy and commit yourself to becoming something special and great. But be leery of blindly following a passion without knowing more about it or where it might lead. Don't chase sparks. Decide if you want to use that spark to build a fire. Once you build that fire, decide if you want to sustain that fire. If your passion shifts, find a way to take the fire you've already built and move it with you to the new location. Don't let the fire you built completely burn out. My passion has shifted over time, but the fire I've built is fuel for the new passion and pursuits because I take the time to move it with me and not blindly follow the next spark.

"Motivation gets you going, but discipline keeps you growing." -John C. Maxwell

The number-one thing I want you to take away from this chapter is that enthusiasm and inspiration can't be your sole source of fuel when trying to achieve greatness. They're unreliable and often won't be there when you want them to. You need to put more stock into discipline, passion, purpose, and commitment if you want to achieve long-term success and not just ride the waves of motivation. I don't want you to completely ignore moments of enthusiasm, inspiration, and desire, however, because when you find yourself feeling this way, you need to set your sails and ride that tailwind as far as it will take you.

Find a balance that utilizes various sources of fuel to keep the fire inside you burning. Anything you can do to keep progressing toward your dreams and goals needs to be considered. If you try to rely solely on excitement, enthusiasm, and inspiration, you won't get there. You have to lean into your discipline. You have to lean into your passion and purpose. You have to combine all of these things to create momentum—like kicking on a surfboard before the wave arrives. Surfers don't just wait for the wave to carry them: they create momentum then ride the wave when it meets them in motion.

Remember, the winds of life direct us through an ocean of possibilities. They will blow periodically throughout each day, but we don't know when or from which direction they'll blow. When the winds do blow, we have to be ready. We have to be disciplined in our approach to preparing for each day. We have to commit ourselves to rowing the boat on the days when the winds don't blow. We have to know where we want to go as well as where we're currently heading. If we do all this, we will eventually find the land we seek.

Ride the winds when they serve you, but don't wait for the days when the winds are strong and at your back. You have to be willing to adjust your sails. You can always paddle to keep the boat moving. You never really know when the winds will shift, but if you're not ready for them you're going to miss the opportunity to make progress. Point the boat where you want to go, set the sails, paddle, and adjust, and you'll find yourself exactly where you're meant to be.

Action Steps:

If you don't know what I'm about to say, it's probably best if you read this chapter one more time. Take action now, today. Pick something you want to achieve and get to work on it. You don't have to finish it, you don't have to make significant progress, you also don't have to have all the steps figured out, but you have to take the first step. Too often we wait around for the right time to do something and that time never comes. Today you will make time for the thing you want in this life. Today you will take action. Don't wait for a tomorrow that isn't promised.

After you've proven you have what it takes to start, then it's all about setting time aside each day to take more action. I'm not worried about planning right now, because if you can't prove that you have what it takes to make a move, all the planning in the world will be for nothing. Today is all about positive steps. Tomorrow you will take another step. Once you've shown you are a person of action, then you can set a day aside to start making some plans, but today you move!

"Discipline is choosing between what you want now and what you want most." -Abraham Lincoln

-Adversity: Finding Strength Amid the Storms-

"The most successful people see adversity not as a stumbling block, but as a stepping stone to greatness." -Shawn Anchor

Everyone faces adversity. It's an unavoidable part of life. Things will be hard for you, in some capacity, at some point during your life. Adversity in some instances will be greater than in others. To be great, you will face even more adversity. That's the thing about success and excellence: the harder the task, the more likely it will be that something will go wrong. If you're reading this and think, "Well, I don't want to achieve greatness" or, "I'll just make sure my goals are less ambitious and I'll avoid adversity," you're wrong. Even if you choose to do nothing with your life, you will still face moments of adversity. You'll get sick, a loved one will die, you'll have an obstacle present itself that you'll have to overcome. So, knowing there is no escape from adversity, why don't we embrace it and all strive for greatness together?

Think of a dream you have. What obstacles have you faced so far on your journey? What obstacles do you think you may face in the future? What problems will you have to solve to realize your dream? I think a lot of time we look at these huge goals and think to ourselves, "I'm going to achieve this because I'm a hard worker and I want it a lot." That's great, but it's also unrealistic. There are thousands of hard workers who never achieve their dreams. Why? I believe it has a lot to do with the adversity they face. I believe they don't overcome the obstacles that arise along the journey because they set the goal and only focus on the future outcome instead of the obstacles that could present themselves along the way.

At the beginning of every journey in our life, I feel we should take time to map out our path, much like we would for a roadtrip across the country. Mark spots along the journey where we want to stop. Mark spots where we may face some tricky stuff. Mark spots that could be defining moments. List obstacles and milestones together so we have a plan for when we might face a moment of difficulty. The more detailed the plan, the better we are prepared to achieve the success we seek.

While writing this part about adversity and mapping out a plan, I found myself thinking back to my first trip to Hawaii. I was in Maui with my wife and, following an early-morning drive to watch the sunrise at the top of the volcano Haleakala, we decided to do a little sightseeing. I took a road that took us around the back side of the island, unaware that we were about to travel the Road to Hana. I just heard there was a cool hike and a waterfall we could see. If you've never been on it, the Road to Hana is basically a one-lane road that winds along the edge of the volcano with blind turns and straight cliff drop-offs. One wide turn and we're sliding down a cliff hundreds of feet into the ocean. And here I am, unprepared in a minivan, trying to survive a road that I didn't know existed.

Obviously, we survived and made it around the island, but I didn't enjoy any of the ride because I was so focused on not falling off a cliff or hitting another car head-on that I couldn't take in any of the sights. Later that vacation, we took a tour that drove the same road in a bus. You would think that would have been terrifying, but knowing what I was getting into and understanding what obstacles lay ahead, I found myself at peace and able to enjoy the beautiful scenery. Had I originally taken the time to plan my route, know where potential scenic stopping points were, and understand what the path held for me, I might have enjoyed my own personal drive along the Road to Hana. Instead, all I wanted to do was get around the island and get back home.

The point of this little side story is that understanding the road you are going to face on your journey can provide you with peace of mind to help you overcome obstacles and adversity when they arise. While this particular adversity was just a drive during a vacation, the principles apply to all of our journeys in life. If we treat our goals and dreams like the first drive and blindly forge ahead, we are bound to face moments we aren't prepared for, and the chance of failure increases. If we take the time to plan our trip and have an understanding of the path we're about to take, however, we will be confident in our ability to succeed in moments of adversity. The journey is still the same, but our state of mind and awareness of what is to come provide us an advantage to overcoming the twists, turns, and cliffs of our life.

"The flower that blooms in adversity is the rarest and most beautiful of all." -Walt Disney

There are few things more challenging in life than watching someone close to you get sick. Following my high school career, my coach, Stephen Gussler, was dealt a blow that would have brought the strongest man to his knees. In 2008, Coach Gussler was diagnosed with stage four colon and rectal cancer. After two years and upward of forty chemo treatments, he was given nine to twelve months to live. This kind of prognosis would bring the most positive and upbeat person in the world into darkness, but not Coach Gussler.

He was given the opportunity to step away from his teaching and coaching duties but kindly declined. He wanted to be around the kids and co-workers who kept him young and focused on the positives instead of chemo and the pain and discomfort of daily life. While battling cancer, Coach Gussler continued to lead and inspire from the front. Even while going through all the chemo and day-to-day discomfort, he inspired his athletes to compete for themselves and each other. He showed them the true power of the human spirit.

The team and the community rallied around Coach Gussler, creating T-shirts and hashtags and holding incredibly powerful rallies to show just how much he was inspiring them. A rallying cry of "GussStrong" could be seen everywhere. Throughout Coach Gussler's battle with cancer, he faced difficult news and hard realities. Expecting to be given a clean bill of health in 2010, the doctors found more cancer; it happened again in 2012.

Even through the harsh and devastating chemo treatments, he continued to show up for his school and team, teaching valuable lessons about life. He taught the entire community of Worthington what it meant to be a servant leader, how to handle adversity head-on, and the power of positivity and joy. Even through the pain and discomfort of cancer, he smiled and joked, saying, "It's a beautiful day to be alive."

He never lost his passion for life and baseball through all of his fight. During the hardest parts of his treatment, he led the Thomas Worthington baseball program to back-to-back conference and district championships. The lessons he taught me and these young men will live on forever, and the power of his resolve was felt across the community.

I still remember an interview in which he said, "Every day is a blessing for me. Many people complain about the daily grind; I look forward to it." These words still stick with me to this day. Coach Gussler was in the middle of a battle for his life in which he was in daily pain and discomfort, and his message was: today is a blessing and let's make it special.

Unfortunately, Coach Stephen Gussler lost his fight with cancer on May 27, 2014. As I sit here writing about this incredible man through tear-filled eyes, I smile knowing how much better and stronger I am for having known him. I'm thankful for the many lessons he taught me and the strength he gave me. I've seen firsthand how to handle adversity head-on with strength and grace. And even though Coach Gussler lost this battle, every person who knew him came out stronger and more equipped to have a life filled with passion and love because of him.

Every day is a gift and a blessing. We are all going to have our difficulties along the way, but the way we see these challenges will define our success and happiness. I encourage all of you to head over to YouTube and watch the fourteen-minute video on the life of Coach Gussler (*https://youtu.be/IEz0GLTPz1k*). Don't let adversity define your life: face your challenges head-on. You have the power to defeat anything if you have the strength to stand up and fight.

"And once the storm is over, you won't remember how you made it through, how you managed to survive. You won't even be sure whether the storm is really over. But one thing is certain. When you come out of the storm,

you won't be the same person who walked in. That's what this storm's all about." -Haruki Murakami

If you take a hard look at your life, I bet you'll find that you've faced adversity quite regularly. Some of the storms are bigger than others. Some of the moments of adversity may not seem like much. It may even be possible that you're not sure how you navigated the adversity. I can think of a couple of big storms and a few light showers from my life. Some of these moments I can tell you exactly how I made it through, and a few others I don't have a clue. I think sometimes when we face adversity head-on as just a small roadblock on the path we're on, we become better at overcoming these obstacles. When we change our mindset about adversity, we can survive a lot, and often we overcome our obstacles without even realizing they were there.

One of the tougher moments of adversity I faced in high school was when I got sick going into junior year. It was during the summer, and I woke up one morning throwing up. Four days later I was still vomiting, even though I hadn't eaten any food in three days. I was to the point where I was throwing up stomach bile. It got so bad that I damaged my esophagus from the stomach acid, which made eating or drinking even more challenging as every time I swallowed it felt like I was swallowing razor blades. At one point I got so bad that my parents took me to the hospital and I took down two IV bags because I was so dehydrated. They did a bunch of tests and sent me home without a real diagnosis, saying that if I vomited again I'd have to come back.

Thankfully, I didn't throw up again, and I slowly began to be able to eat ice chips. After ten days of being sick, I finally was at a point where I could eat small bits of food. Even though the virus or infection had passed, I was so weak and had lost around 40 pounds. I don't remember how exactly I turned the corner or what finally helped me to become better, but I do remember standing in front of the mirror looking at my once athletic body, which now resembled that of a frail, malnourished child from one of those sponsor-a-third-world-country commercials.

I was so weak that walking up the stairs made me winded. I remember returning to the gym with my friend and struggling to bench press 95 pounds when prior to being sick I was benching over 200 pounds with relative ease. I had lost more than half of my strength and 20 percent of my size. It was a real low point in my life. I had always been a strong and powerful athlete, and now I could hardly do anything without feeling exhausted—if I could even do it at all. I spent the remainder of the summer working out and trying to get my weight back up. I rededicated myself to my performance as an athlete. Through this difficult time, I became stronger mentally because I had to fight for everything again. I was back to my first days of lifting weights with a memory of who I used to be fresh in my mind.

I had to battle the disappointment of failure every day as I tried to find my way back to the athlete I once was. During this time I also began to compete again as a baseball player. It was hard not being able to run as fast, throw as hard, or hit with any power or consistency. The bat felt heavy in my hands, the balls I used to snap across the infield now one-hopped to the first baseman. But over time I started to get my weight back up. My strength and speed returned, and as the school year started, I felt like I was almost back to my usual self. The only real difference was that I was battle-tested and hardened from having to overcome the struggles of a summer of regrowth. I had a new appreciation for being strong and healthy. I worked harder than ever and became a better version of myself from the challenges I faced during that time.

I don't believe it was a coincidence that my junior year of high school was also an extremely successful year. It was my first year being recognized as All-Conference and All-District for baseball. It was also the year I was asked to be part of junior Team Ohio for a summer tournament. I believe I had what it took to be successful, but this moment of challenge provided me the internal strength I needed to focus on becoming great. I worked out harder, I did extra hitting and fielding. I was trying to get back to my old level of strength and skill, but this work allowed me to surpass it.

I relate my illness and situation to what Michael Jordan faced when he didn't make his varsity team as a sophomore. While I wasn't cut from a team, I did face an adversity that forced me to make a decision. Following that adversity, we both rededicated ourselves to our sport and to becoming the best version of ourselves that we could. Obviously, he found a whole other gear and became the greatest player ever, but we both created success from our struggles. These struggles are sometimes necessary to provide us the opportunity to come back stronger. Adversity is the pressure that creates diamonds. The more adversity/pressure we face, the stronger we become over time.

"Your hardest times often lead to the greatest moments of your life. Keep going. Tough situations build strong people in the end." -Roy T. Bennet

During the fall and winter of 2017, I was working as the strength and conditioning coach for the

Pickerington Central softball team. They were working hard preparing for the upcoming season in which there were some high expectations for them. The girls had been putting in hard work with me for a couple of months when one day I was training them and the head coach didn't show up. I didn't think anything of it, but when I showed up the next workout day and she wasn't there again, I began to wonder what was going on.

Apparently, there was an investigation happening and the coach was asked to step down from her position. I'm not going to get into the details of the reason for her being fired, but know that it was sudden, unexpected, and emotionally challenging for a lot of these girls to handle. This team, which had a tradition of competitive excellence and championship performances, was now stuck in the middle of their off-season without a coach. Not only were they stuck without a coach, they were battling feelings of anger, hurt, and betrayal.

I continued to show up each day for workouts and attempted to put some of the older girls into leadership positions to take charge, as it was their team now. The team was left stranded, floating in the middle of the ocean without a paddle or compass to point them in the right direction. As high school kids, I can't imagine how lost they probably felt. They were staring adversity squarely in the eye. It wasn't until right before the start of the season that a replacement coach was chosen. I came on as an assistant to help bridge the gap between the new coach and the team with whom I had built relationships during this time.

Over the course of the season, the adversity they faced became a rallying cry for them. The betrayal and pain of the loss of their coach became a bond that held the team together. It was quite possibly the closest team I have ever coached. They loved each other, they trusted each other, and they battled each day for the sister next to them. It was a special group to be a part of. This group taught me how strong a group can become by facing difficult times together.

By the end of the season, this team had become conference runner-up and made an appearance in the district championship game. While the season ended with a loss in the championship game, the journey to get there speaks to the resilience this team had. We never backed down from a challenge. We stuck by each other and battled all the way to the end.

In the second round of the tournament, facing Hilliard Darby, we won an epic shootout on the road against a significantly higher-seeded team. The game was a back-and-forth battle. We took an early lead 4-1 into the bottom of the third, where we surrendered the lead 5-4. The following half inning we tied the game back up.

In the fifth inning we exploded for five runs only to turn around and give up five runs in the bottom half. We took the lead in the sixth and expanded it in the seventh inning, going into the bottom half of the inning leading 14-10. We had a freshman pitcher on the mound to face the middle of Darby's line up. After a walk and a strikeout, the fifth batter in Darby's lineup crushed a home run to center field and the game was now 14-12. The pressure was mounting as the next hitter got hit by a pitch and now the tying run was coming to bat. My girls never backed down. With the pressure mounting and Darby gaining momentum, my team banded together to get the next batter to ground out and end the game with a strikeout.

The next game was against Watkins Memorial and was the exact opposite of the game with Hilliard Darby. It was a ten-inning pitchers' duel. We had struggled to put the ball in play all game, striking out nineteen times going into the top of the tenth. We had only had two hits to this point in the game, but the top of our order was up and we still carried hope with us. Even after our lead-off hitter of the inning struck out, the energy in our dugout never waned. The next hitter up was Taylor Whalen, who was 0 for 3 on the day with three strikeouts. It just takes one, and with a 1 ball, 1 strike count she singled to center field.

We were in business. Our best hitter, Zoie Smith, was coming up with a runner on base in the top of the tenth. Even though she was 0 for 4 on the day, she was just as confident as she was at the start of the game. Zoie took the first pitch for a ball, then sent the second pitch of the at-bat soaring over the center field fence. The bench and stands erupted as she rounded the bases. We added another run with a home run by Cami Fisk before the inning ended, and we were taking a 3-0 lead into the bottom of the tenth.

This game wasn't over, though, and we knew we had to battle through the top of this tough Watkins lineup one more time. The inning started with two singles in a row. The tying run would be coming to the plate for the middle of the Watkins order, which consisted of several strong power hitters. After a strikeout, the third hitter in the Watkins lineup singled to center, scoring their first run of the game. The winning run was now coming to the plate. After a flukey play, we got an out on the runner advancing to third for the second out of the inning, then finished the game on a weak ground ball to the third baseman.

We ended up losing in the championship game 2-0 despite an epic effort from my girls. They battled all game long to the last out. In the final inning we got two runners on and our captain and team leader Cami Fisk was up with two outs. On the first pitch of her at-bat, she crushed a ball to left field that soared over the fence just foul. It was probably just a few feet from being fair. Two pitches later, she put a ball in play and it was caught by the right fielder. It was a tragic ending to an incredible run.

Taking on adversity doesn't guarantee you're going to win. It doesn't mean the final result is going to be what you hope and dream for. Often the adversity will win, but it's through the difficult moments that you become more than you were before. I have no doubt these girls are stronger for the adversity they faced in that season. The final set of games is proof enough to me, but in the years to follow I watched these girls move on through their high school and into their college careers with confidence and belief in themselves. They continued to perform and shine in the most pressure-packed situations. That season, and the adversity they faced, will serve them beyond their time as softball players and well into their adult lives. It's a team I'll never forget and I'm forever grateful to have been a part of.

"It is your reaction to adversity, not the adversity itself, that determines how your life's story will develop."
-Dieter F. Uchtdorf

I believe we are hardwired to face adversity. In a sense, we are also wired to seek adversity. We're drawn in by the challenges that are presented by facing our demons. It is in these most difficult moments that our story is truly developed. All great moments of triumph come from moments of adversity. Think for a moment of compelling stories and usually they have to do with overcoming adversity. We are drawn to adversity just like we're drawn to stories of people overcoming adversity. Think of any movie you loved as a kid; odds are, the hero overcame great adversity.

I'm a huge movie fan, and I love stories of triumph or when the underdog faces adversity head-on. Stories like *Miracle* (the story of the 1980 U.S. hockey team), *Rocky*, *Rudy*, and *Spider-Man*. Each of these stories are about an individual or group overcoming adversity. *Miracle* centers around a group of amateur hockey players who have to compete against the greatest hockey powerhouse in world history in the Olympics of 1980. This story shows their struggles to find their identity and gel before becoming eventual gold medalists. *Rocky* is a great story of a down-on-his-luck boxer whose whole life is filled with adversity. What makes Rocky even more compelling is we can relate to the struggles he's going through, and it draws us into his future and eventual success. *Rudy* is the story of Rudy Ruettiger, a walk-on at Notre Dame. Rudy is another incredible underdog story. He's undersized, poor, struggles with school, and makes it solely on his heart and grit. Last is Spider-Man. I'm sure some of you may be thinking, "What adversity does he overcome?" But he is completely shaped into the hero he is by adversity: the death of his Uncle Ben. Without this adversity, Peter Parker may never have become the Spider-Man we know and love.

We love these stories because on some level we can all relate to them. We can all relate to facing an opponent deemed impossible to defeat. We've all had tough times and been down on our luck like Rocky. Tough times are part of everyone's life at some point, though maybe not to the level Rocky experienced. We've all felt like the odds were completely against us like Rudy. Been told we're too small, too slow, not the right person for the job, or wasting our time. To see Rudy succeed makes us believe we, too, might succeed. And everyone reading this book has dealt with the loss of a loved one. This one connects us to a superhuman that we otherwise would not see as human. The human aspect and struggle bring us in.

All of these stories are compelling because of their adversity. Their final achievements matter more because of the obstacles they were forced to overcome. So next time you find yourself staring into the eyes of adversity, remember that it is just a moment in your journey. In fact, it could potentially be the defining moment of your story, the moment that makes your success more compelling. Embrace that moment; lean into it. When you emerge on the other side you will be changed by it, you will be redefined by it, and you'll be stronger because of it.

The reason I feel this is important for us to understand is that we will all overcome some adversity on our way to being great. Adversity is unavoidable. By knowing this and appreciating that our journey is going to face adversity, we can shift from trying to avoid it to deciding how to overcome it. When we make this shift from feeling sorry for our difficulties to expecting them and focusing on what we do next, we allow ourselves to solve the problem created by our adversity. This allows us to become stronger from our struggles, not defined or defeated by them.

The interesting thing about adversity is we've all been thrust into the middle of great adversity over the year and a half of the COVID-19 pandemic. The entire world has been impacted by this disease. Millions of people have died. Thousands of jobs and homes have been lost. And whether or not you were personally affected by this disease, you know somebody who has been.

None of us were looking for it or prepared for it, but it showed up and challenged us all the same. During this time, there have been those who blame their situation on the pandemic and those who have used their situation to make something more of themselves. I've seen stories of people facing hard times and losing the battle with adversity (sometimes with their lives, unfortunately), but I've seen others take this pandemic and make something new of themselves. I personally have chosen to branch out and try new things. I started a podcast, I finished a book that I started writing in college (and now finally have it published), I wrote blog posts, and now I'm writing this book.

My point is this, during adverse times there are many easy options available to us. It's the difficult choices, or the hard options, that lead to increased success. It's doing the difficult work, pursuing the unknown strategy, or doing the work when nobody is watching that defines our true character. I've always been the type of person that puts in work whether someone is watching me or not. I love the work. I love purposeful work. I love detailed and difficult work. The hardest thing for me during this time is finding good, quality work to keep me busy. But I'm always looking for something. I'm always searching for new ways to improve and better myself. No matter what the future holds or what adversity I may face, my progress toward improvement will stay consistent.

As you continue to read this book, I implore you to seek out new ways of doing things. To be open to change. To be adaptable to whatever life throws at you. To learn, grow, and develop as a person and leader. Don't look at the things that have been taken from you, but instead search for the new door that is available to you. No matter what your situation and no matter how many doors were shut, if you search hard enough, a new door is waiting for you to walk through. You just have to be willing to look, and then once you find it, be brave enough to open it.

There will always be challenges in your life. There will always be some kind of adversity you'll be asked to confront. Take time to sharpen the tools in your tool box. Enhance your skills and prepare yourself for future challenges. Change the way you see adversity, change the way you handle difficult moments, and forge into the unknown without fear. Be courageous, be bold, and try new things. Most importantly, don't wait for things to return to normal: create a new normal. Create a new you—a better, stronger, more resilient you. While you weather this storm, continue to grow, and when the seas settle and the rain subsides, you will emerge more prepared for what's beyond the storm.

No matter how hard you try, you are going to face adversity. So, with that in mind, why would you try to avoid it? Seek greatness and challenge and expect adversity along the way. Each challenging moment is a cornerstone of the person you will eventually become. The world is difficult, and moments of challenge are everywhere. Face them head-on. Walk, unwavering, into the storm. There may be times that seem as if the storm will never end, but know if you just keep moving, this, too, shall pass. Dream big and be bold: the challenge you face today will open you up to a world of great success tomorrow!

Action Steps:

This is another reflection chapter. You've been dealt blows in your life, some bigger than others. Each of these blows was a test. Each of those tests was about overcoming adversity. What have you overcome to be where you are? What have you been through that makes you stronger and more prepared? Are you ready for the next challenge that's bound to show up? Understand that you are more resilient than you think. You have what it takes to weather any storm.

There are bound to be more challenges in your life. The greater the goals you set for yourself, the more adversity you'll eventually have to face. By understanding what you've overcome to this point, you will be better prepared for the future difficulties you're bound to face. You are stronger than you think. You have what it takes to be resilient and navigate the storms of life. Take account of all you've accomplished and let that fuel you as you set out for bigger and better things.

"Strength doesn't come from what you can do. It comes from overcoming the things you once thought you couldn't." -Rikki Rogers

-Grit: The Secret Sauce-

"Grit is sticking with your future day in, day out, and not just for the week, not just for the month, but for years." -Angela Duckworth

I think one of the reasons I have chosen to write this book is to test my grit. I believe myself to be gritty, but sometimes I wonder if I really am as gritty as I believe? I think this is probably a common feeling, because while I tend to follow through on things and commit myself to long-term goals and endeavors, I haven't to this point in my life achieved all that I hope to. Is that because I lack grit? Or is it because it has not been long enough to achieve my desired goals? My belief is that the latter is the reason. I also believe that writing this book moves me closer to my aspirations to help others and be seen as a knowledgeable coach. Lastly, I believe this book tests my grit and shows me that I'm capable of finishing difficult things.

The last part is the most important to me because I don't believe I'll ever be satisfied with the number of people I help or the level of knowledge I gather as a coach. But by testing my grit and showing myself that I can finish what I start, I'm opening myself up to future possibilities that come from being gritty. The completion of this project will be a milestone for me on my path to greatness. It will challenge me on a number of the topics I write about in this book. I will have to work hard daily over a stretch of days. I will face adversity and setbacks along the way. I will have to commit myself to the process and display my grit. In the end, whether this book hits home for everyone or not, I'll have developed a new set of skills and abilities that will allow me to thrive in future situations.

Grit may be the most important attribute in determining future success. As I mentioned before, this book is not set up in any particular order, and no one word or chapter carries more weight than the others, because if you are lacking in any area you'll fall short of your goals and aspirations. But I do believe grit carries a lot of weight because it contains a number of the other characteristics within it.

"Over time, grit is what separates fruitful lives from aimlessness." -John Ortberg

I believe grit is the secret weapon of the successful. It's the secret weapon that gives them an advantage over their competitors and allows them to continue on through the most difficult times. Grit is the ability to hold onto a dream longer and keep working toward a goal through extreme adversity despite what the world around you may be saying. It's a belief in yourself that you have what it takes to be successful and that no matter what obstacles stand in your way, you will overcome, eventually. Grit is the secret sauce: Those who have it will eventually achieve the success they seek. Those who don't will find themselves chasing those who do. To be great, we must embrace the long road ahead, and we must become grittier than those who aim to stop us.

When I hear the word "grit," I immediately get the vision of an athlete beaten down by their training. They're on the floor, sweat dripping from their face. Dirt streaks mixed with sweat cover their clothes and are smeared across their face. They look like they've given all they can and have nothing left. Then you see them grimace and push themselves to their feet, take a breath, and find a way to get back to work. They are at a place where most people would quit, but something inside them spurs them on to want to give more, to want to endure more. They have a vision of something greater and know that the only way to get there is through hell. And they're willing to take that path.

What makes a person continue when they've been pushed beyond what most humans can endure? What gives someone the strength to continue on in the face of insurmountable odds? Grit isn't just about physical perseverance, though. Think about what it takes to achieve excellence over your lifetime. Think about the endurance it takes to show up every day and try something new, to fail, to continue to put blood, sweat, and tears into a vision you have that nobody believes in. Would you be able to stay true to what you believe in the face of consistent failure and ridicule from others? Would you be able to see your future and know that all the failed efforts and work today is for that, no matter what those around you believe or say?

When you see someone who's successful, what are your first thoughts? How many times have you seen a great athlete and muttered under your breath, "Well, they're just gifted"? Or seen a great work of art and thought, "I could never do that; they're just artsy"? Or seen an awesome invention and thought, "I wish I were that smart"? We often get drawn into this cycle of wishing we were capable of someone else's great achievements. We look at their end result and forget that they put in hours of work behind the scenes to become the person we see. Often, this leads to resentment or disgust toward that person, or even excuses as to why we aren't as successful as they are. Every person is capable of achieving greatness and success, but few people grasp what it takes to get there. It comes down to finding our passion and being just a little more gritty.

Why does grit determine success more than any other character trait? Why is talent not more important? I've found that talent is often overused and misunderstood. Is a young kid who's bigger than his peers more talented or just genetically ahead at this moment? So often we tell a kid they're talented, or gifted, or special, and then we fail to push them to continue to develop. Then, when the time comes that they're finally tested—and in order to be great, we will all be tested—they crumble. Life's challenges test us to determine whether we're truly committed to doing what it takes to be successful. When they do, we don't have the determination and resolve to overcome them. Grit is defined by Merriam-Webster as "firmness of mind or spirit: unyielding courage in the face of hardship or danger." Grit is that stubbornness in all of us to stick with something until we get it right. It's that part of us that holds onto a belief that we can achieve something when everyone else in the world is saying it's impossible. It's the willingness to get back up after every time we're knocked down.

When I think of grit, I often find myself thinking of Navy SEALs. Partly because cinema paints them as complete badasses and partly because only 25 percent of recruits accepted into SEAL training make it all the way through. If that's not the definition of grit, I don't know what is. When training starts, every recruit scores similarly on mental aptitude, vision, physical fitness, and a number of other standards. These are the best of the best the Navy has to offer, yet only 25 percent of all recruits survive. Why? Because when faced with adversity, when pushed to the limit, when faced with hardship and daily stress, both mentally and physically, only those truly passionate, committed, and gritty come out on the other side. If you only like the idea of becoming a SEAL, you won't survive. Now, I'm not a soldier and I've never been through SEAL training, but if the reason recruits make it through isn't more talent, a higher IQ, better vision, more athleticism, or being lucky or gifted, what is the difference?

Grit allows us to push onward when the world says to stop. When the critics say you can't or you shouldn't, the passion we have for our goals and the determination to see them through will carry us forward. Grit also allows us to hold onto long-term goals when others can't see what we're working for. That vision of what we want to be or create, and the passion we have to create it, can be lost on others. They will doubt you and tell you you're wasting your time and it can't be done, but our grit allows us to ignore those people, to forge on and continue down the path we know will get us there. When I think of this ability to envision what we want, I often find myself thinking of the works of Michelangelo.

Did you know it took him two years to create the statue of David? It took him another four years to do the Sistine Chapel. Imagine walking past him working on the statue of David six months into its creation and seeing a block of marble chipped at and vaguely in the shape of a person. Would you share Michelangelo's vision of what was being created? Would you have the steely reserve to continue to pound the stone every day, sometimes seeing no change in the piece in front of you? Would you have the patience to move slowly and cautiously every day, knowing that one mistake and all the work you put in would be wasted? There's not exactly an "undo last move" button when it comes to marble. Could you put all your attention into one single detail until it becomes exactly how you want it? Do you have enough grit?

"Grit is guts, resilience, industriousness, and tenacity. Grit is the ability to focus, stay determined, stay optimistic in the face of a challenge, and simply work harder than the next guy or gal." -Linda Kaplan Thaler

Read that quotation again. As you can see, grit is complex. There are a number of moving parts that create grit. Grit gives you courage to face your fears. Grit is the motivation you need to continue working when odds seem insurmountable. Grit allows you to ignore the naysayers and critics. Grit allows you to face adversity and continue on the path, knowing you will eventually succeed. Grit is the determination and fortitude to work harder than anyone else until you achieve your dreams.

As you can see, grit has some serious power when it comes to achieving success. The question, then, is how do we harness the power of grit? Is grit something that can be created? How do we become like the greats and develop this ability to achieve success through adversity? I think a huge part of becoming gritty starts with our ability to finish what we start. I think no matter the task, teaching our mind and body to finish gives us confidence that we have what it takes to win. Even if what we're doing doesn't affect our future goals or dreams, this consistency in finishing what we start teaches our minds to focus and see things through.

The second big part of unlocking your grit is finding what you're passionate about. When we believe so deeply in what we're doing or pursuing, we have deeper strength to navigate the hard times. A lot of people quit when things get hard because they aren't passionate about what they're doing. Think about it. People don't quit because things are too easy; they quit because things are hard. And when faced with adversity and the difficult parts of getting better, they decide the work isn't worth the end result. The passion for the path isn't there. You must want to succeed more than you care about how long it takes, or how much it hurts, or who thinks you can't do it. What dream are you chasing that you care that much about?

When you think back to some of the stories I referenced in the chapter on adversity, it isn't just the adversity our heroes face that captivates us. It's the grit they display in the face of adversity. Adversity is just the catalyst that allows us to demonstrate our grit. Without adversity we don't get to fully tap into our grit and overcome the situations we find ourselves in.

However, it isn't just the adversity that leads us to success, it's the grit we display in those moments. One doesn't work without the other. To achieve long-lasting success we will face adversity, but we also must display grit. The two together allow us to develop the tools to achieve and then sustain success.

Once you tap into the power of grit, anything is possible. The dreams you have for yourself can become a reality. You now possess the power to overcome any obstacle that may stand in the way of your dreams. Grit will power you through the difficult moments so you might one day experience the view from atop the mountain. This ability to forge on, face setbacks as learning opportunities, and believe in your process gives you an advantage on the competition. Developing your grit is truly a superpower, one that can provide you with the necessary tools to solve any of life's obstacles on the way to success. So, challenge yourself, put yourself in difficult situations, and follow through on the tasks you wish to accomplish. If you're looking to discover more about your grit, I highly recommend reading *Grit: The Power of Passion and Perseverance* by Angela Duckworth.

Action Steps:

There are two things I believe are crucial in helping to develop more grit. The first is finishing the things you start. No matter how much you want to quit, don't let yourself. The ability to finish despite wanting to stop will harden your resolve and develop more grit. Get in the habit of finishing things now, and hold others accountable for finishing what they start as well. Try your best to not start on something new until you finish what you're currently working on. I'm guilty of this; it's easy to make an excuse for why you didn't finish when you're starting something else.

The second part of this is to discover your passion. The more passionate you are about something, the easier it is to stick with things. You have to practice sticking to it, but that will serve you well once you discover your passion. Then you'll have the skills developed through finishing things you're less passionate about, combined with a newfound passion, to fuel you through the hard work required to succeed.

Grit isn't something you can just acquire overnight. It must be earned over time. It's a combination of stubbornness, resilience, focus, determination, and stick-to-it-iveness. All of these take time to develop and master. It starts with your internal refusal to quit what you start and the search for your passion. Once you've done that, you'll find some of these other attributes begin to show up more regularly.

"Grit is the stubborn refusal to quit." -Jonah Lehrer

94

-Curiosity Didn't Kill the Cat; It Helped Him Achieve Greatness-

"I have no special talent. I am only passionately curious." -Albert Einstein

I was always naturally curious. I explored my surroundings as a child, looking at the world in different ways. As I got older and began to compete in athletics, that curiosity led me to look for ways to compete at a higher level and find playing time. I was always looking for an advantage or a way I could get a leg up on my competition. I'm not sure where this curiosity came from, but I definitely utilized it to my advantage.

The way I looked at basketball was that there were only so many shots in a given game, and those had to be distributed between the number of scorers on the floor. There is no limit on the number of plays where defense is needed, however: it's constant. By being a player who focused on defense, I would always have a spot on the floor. I used my defense to create offense for myself. Early in my playing career, 80 percent of my points came off of steals for layups. The other 20 percent came off of offensive rebounds.

While the rest of the basketball world was focused on creating their own shots and being scorers, I focused on the areas that others didn't spend as much time working on but were still vital to the team. I was never the tallest player but often led my team in rebounds. I wasn't the fastest player but would anticipate the game and get at least a few fast-break steal layups each game. I looked at the game of basketball from a different place, and my curiosity led me down a unique path.

It wasn't until the last several years, though, that I fully began to embrace and appreciate my curiosity. As a player it was there, but I didn't understand it. I didn't know how to use it. As a coach and someone who is constantly looking to learn more, these days I lean into my curiosity. I ask more questions than I ever did. I look for chances to explore areas that others ignore. Much like when I was a young basketball player obsessed with playing great defense because I knew it gave me the best chance to get on the court, I am constantly looking for something that makes me stand out from the crowd.

The world rewards curiosity. Those who ask questions and seek answers become leaders and innovators in their field. If you can look at your situation from a different place than the rest of the world, you can begin to unlock new ways of seeing the world. If you're willing to fail, you may stumble upon a secret to success others around you will ignore. We're genetically wired to be curious, but throughout our lives we learn to stop asking questions and follow the crowd. It's time to deprogram that mindset and explore the world in a new and different way.

Start questioning the world. Not from a place of defiance or malice, but from a place of genuine curiosity and seeking clarity. If you're genuinely seeking knowledge and understanding through questioning and curiosity, you will begin to unlock a new appreciation for information and knowledge and how you can apply it to various situations. It starts with an open mind: admitting you're going to be wrong often and that you're a lifelong learner on a quest for more knowledge. You're not looking to solve the world's problems today, but to seek knowledge for application to a potential problem in the future.

"Curiosity, I think, is the most important quality you can have. With curiosity you figure things out. You're always looking for ways to get better or always looking for reasons why certain things work. That curiosity leads you to knowledge." -Kobe Bryant

How often do you ask why? How much do you question in this world? Are you seeking new knowledge or stuck with the old adages, "My way or the highway" or, "This is how we've always done it"? I think this is a commonly misunderstood characteristic of those who achieve high levels of success. It's often believed that highly successful people, whether in business or sport, are stubborn. While they may display stubbornness in some areas of their lives, that stubbornness doesn't trickle into their quest for greatness. The best look at every situation as a learning opportunity. This curiosity keeps them searching for the next edge in their development.

The ability to question things allows you to be in a constant state of learning. One of my favorite things I hear people say about Michael Jordan and Kobe Bryant relates to their constant quest for more knowledge. They looked beyond basketball for every advantage they could find. They were curious about training, mindfulness, film study, leadership, and wanted to learn from everyone who was successful. It didn't matter if nobody had ever done that before; honestly, that made it more intriguing to them. Their desire to learn more than everyone else in the game was part of their unique makeup that allowed them to be great.

I have two young children. Each day I watch them explore their new world. They are experiencing the world around them for the first time. They analyze each situation and test their environment and their limits. My kids will try to figure out toys and how they work. They are curious about foods, animals, plants, people, and their abilities. My younger child watches my oldest do things, and you can see the inquisitiveness in her eyes. She studies how he does things and is learning right before my eyes. My son climbs and jumps, runs and falls, constantly testing his limits and displaying curiosity about what he can accomplish. I watch him lining up jumps from the couch to the ottoman, calculating things in his mind, then taking the leap.

We're hardwired to be curious. We're wired to explore and test our environment. Have you ever watched a child closely? If you have, you can see them curiously exploring their new world like my kids do. They touch everything, they study it closely and even put it in their mouths (probably not something you want to do). They look at the world without prejudice or bias. Everything is new and must be explored, examined, and sampled. Through sampling, a child learns what each new object in their world does and how it works. This innate curiosity leads to incredible growth during the early development years.

As kids get older and start to communicate, they continue their curiosity by going through a phase of questioning. "What's that?" and, "Why?" become a kid's favorite words. Their quest for understanding and their constant questioning spark another phase of learning. Yet somehow we forget that our curiosity is the key to our development and eventually push back against questioning. At some point we are told to stop questioning and don't talk back. The quest for an explanation and deeper meaning is denied, and we eventually drift away from being curious toward being compliant. We start to accept the answers given to us by people of authority, and the curiosity that sparked our initial intellectual growth dissipates.

The ability to look at the world through a lens of curiosity is special. Too many people today get closed off to trying new things or exploring new paths.

Somewhere along the way we lose the curious nature that we're born with. The point at which we stop being curious is different for everyone, and not everyone is discouraged from questioning, but usually at some point we're told not to question authority or the way things are done, and we comply. We stop exploring new ideas and taking risks that may not work because we're concerned we may be reprimanded or we worry about what others may think. Once we lose our curiosity, we lose our ability to question, and we ultimately slow our ability to grow. The world is designed for us to question things. Be curious and explore!

"Millions saw the apple fall, but Newton asked why."
-Bernard Baruch

I recently read a book by Adam Grant called *Think Again* that is all about curiosity. It talks about looking at the world and its problems through the lens of a scientist and being willing to question the results and current beliefs without bias. It is also about being able to re-examine your current beliefs when new information is presented. Can you change your mind as you learn more, or are you stuck believing in things that have been proven wrong?

I think this is an important lesson for those out there seeking knowledge. If you accept that everything you think you know is temporary and can change, you allow yourself to remain curious about new information. This opens you up to challenging your current beliefs and seeing new information through an inquisitive lens. Ultimately, this allows us to accept new information and apply it to current beliefs. It sounds easy, but changing your mind is very challenging. Even when presented with a strong argument against our current beliefs, we tend to hold onto them and deny the new information.

The best allow themselves to remain curious. They don't get sucked into the common misconception that they know it all. They accept that they don't have all the answers and that their quest for knowledge is never-ending. The best are also willing to try new things or change their way of thinking. The best don't get stuck in the mindset of "this is how we've always done it." There is a willingness to be different. The best are always looking for something to give them an advantage.

By being open to change and willing to try new things, we allow ourselves to question what we know and explore unknown solutions. Did you know that when Michael Jordan first started weight training, he would work out on game days? This may not seem like a big deal now, but when he first started doing that, nobody else was working out on game days. This was something unique to him, and everyone told him it wasn't the right way to do it. However, Jordan was open to being different. He was open to trying something new. He was curious.

Obviously, the rest is history for Jordan as he went on to become a legend. I bet if you were to explore many of the world's incredible innovations and technological advances, they came from people who were willing to try new things. People willing to walk the unbeaten path and curiously explore the world tend to stumble upon solutions that nobody else knew were there. Don't just follow the crowd; they might be marching in the wrong direction.

I think a lot of the time we become a product of those who taught us. This is why we tend to repeat the mistakes of the past or do things "like we've always done." We are also drawn to follow others and not stand out in a crowd. Not everyone wants to be walking the path alone, but if we want to discover something new or that gives us an advantage, we have to be willing to stand alone at times and try something different.

It's time to start looking at the world through children's eyes. Instead of taking biases of the world around us into a situation, view everything as if it's the first time. Question things and explore potential new ways. I'm not saying to ignore the teachings of the past, but don't be afraid to challenge a theory. Don't be afraid to take that knowledge and apply it in a different way. Take time to be different and explore what could be out there. Remember, if Christopher Columbus wasn't curious, he would have never explored the seas and discovered the new world.

I hope you all begin to seek more knowledge. I hope you begin to look at things from a different perspective. Don't be afraid of being seen as different or wrong. Remember, most things we appreciate today were once seen as something that was never done before or wrong. Even bikes and automobiles were seen as impractical when they were invented. The home computer, iPhone, iPod, laptop, lightbulb, and even calculators were seen as unnecessary and never-going-to-work inventions. Be bold, be curious, take risks, and explore the world through eyes that question everything.

Action Steps:

Look at the world through an unbiased filter. See things as what they are—constantly evolving—and be willing to explore new information. This will be hard, as you will naturally want to defend what you believe. Curiosity is about exploring various ways of doing things. It's about questioning things, even if you currently believe them as truth or the way. A fun drill might be to pretend you're preparing for a debate and you have to convince yourself of the opposite side of your belief. Could you present a compelling argument?

The other thing I want is to see everyone reading this book try doing something different than everyone else. Explore something different than what people believe is the "right" way. Be open to being wrong. It's OK to have strong beliefs and convictions, but don't be blind to seeing the world around you for what it is. Find strong evidence to support your beliefs, but really listen to the other side and try to do so without bias toward your current view or beliefs.

Curiosity is challenging. Everyone is trying to convince us that their way is the truth, and if you don't pick a side, you become outcast or vilified. Be strong and remain curious about the world. Question everything. Be willing to change as new evidence is presented. Be willing to fail. The world needs curious people. We need people to question the way of things and to explore new and innovative ways. Remain childlike in how you see the world, as if it's your first time!

"Curiosity is the most powerful thing you own." -James Cameron

-Know Thyself-

"Self-awareness gives you the capacity to learn from your mistakes as well as your successes. It enables you to keep growing." -Lawrence Bossidy

I'd like to believe I've always had a pretty solid grasp on who I am, but then again, I could be way off. That's the hard part of self-reflection and self-awareness. I want to believe I'm being honest about who I am, but early on I didn't ask for help figuring out who I am from others, so it's possible I was misled on my quest. That being said, I've spent a lot of time throughout my years as a player, coach, and business owner reflecting on who I am. It is through this reflection that I believe I have a solid understanding of who I am today.

More recently I've decided to include others on my quest to find out who I am. I try to ask people who know me well but aren't so close that they feel the need to tell me what I want to hear. I need the honest, hard truth about who I am if I'm going to improve. I need to know my areas of weakness if I'm going to strengthen them. We must face our shortcomings head-on if we're going to improve. Self-awareness allows me to be confident in my strengths and aware of my weaknesses so I can attack any situation and win.

Through my conversations and self-reflection I've come to believe in myself as a leader. My leadership works best, however, in an assistant role. I've done my best leading and educating as an assistant. I am confident I could be a strong head coach or leader, but when I'm in a supporting role I feel I shine. Not because the pressure of being in charge is too much, but because I do best with direction. I'm a person who needs a list of things planned out for me, but I'm not great at making that list myself.

As an assistant I know my role. I'm in charge of specific areas and I have a task that I must execute. Having that direction allows me to really focus on teaching and leading as an extension of the head coach or boss. When I'm in this position, it frees me up from worrying about what everyone else is doing or the direction of the whole group. I can still be allowed to lead, but I'm following a plan already put in place. I tend to get so focused on specific tasks that I lose sight of the whole.

It took me a while to figure this out. I always thought I wanted to be a head coach. I guess some part of me would still love to have my own program at some point, but I'm not in a hurry to make that happen. It's more important for me to find a coach I believe in and a culture that I want to be a part of and join a strong team. That is how I felt when I was coaching with Ray Noe and Jenny Young.

As a member of the Pickerington Central (a high school program in Pickerington, Ohio) baseball coaching staff, Ray allowed me to utilize my strengths with autonomy. I was tasked with working with the pitchers my first year, and we developed a strategy to prepare them to warm up and enter the game ready to go. Ray left me to develop this all on my own and never injected himself into the things I was trying to accomplish. He asked questions, but never dictated what I was to do. We developed some great mental strategies that we then added to other players as the season went on.

The next year we brought in a pitching coach, which was great because I'm not a pitching coach, and I was tasked to work more with the infielders and hitters alongside Ray. During this time, I played to my strength of understanding mental performance, and it allowed us to develop one of the best hitting teams I've ever been around. Again, Ray allowed me to coach without trying to tell me what to do, and I knew myself enough to pick my places to interject and add value. It was a great team, in part due to the staff that Ray assembled and the freedom he gave everyone to coach to their strengths.

When I switched over to softball to coach with Jenny Young, I again got more freedom. Jenny knew how to lean on my strengths as a coach (relationship building and mental performance strategies). She put me in charge of team-building activities, and when we needed a specific kind of pep talk, she knew I had to be the one to deliver it. We worked very well together, and I was able to grow even more as a coach.

Give me a task and watch me go to work. I'm the same way at home, which I'm sure fires up my wife. If you put a list together, I'll knock it out, but if you give me vague direction about "cleaning up the house" or something like that, good luck. I need structure. I need a plan and an order in which to attack the day. The more planned out my day, the more productive I become. I don't do well with large amounts of free time and a lot of things to accomplish.

"Self-awareness is the ability to take an honest look at your life without any attachment to it being right or wrong, good or bad." -Debbie Ford

Something that has become extremely apparent to me during my study and communication with high performers is the importance of self-awareness. The people who achieve high levels of success or excellence tend to have a better understanding of who they are than those who don't. There is value in knowing who you are, what you know, and what you don't. When you start to think about self-awareness, it has to start with an honest assessment of where you currently are. Lay out your strengths and weaknesses.

What makes self-awareness challenging is that everyone thinks they're self-aware. There's not a person I've ever talked to who openly says they don't know who they are. Everyone claims to be self-aware, but few truly understand what that means. So how do we fix this problem? How do we begin to assess what we don't know? Because in the words of Socrates, "You don't know what you don't know."

I believe there are two places to start to give you a stronger understanding of who you are. The first is to locate a few friends or colleagues you can trust to give you honest feedback and ask them to evaluate who you are. Give each of these people a list of questions you want answered, making sure to give them all the same set of questions. Then you can compile a list of responses and compare them to what you think.

A few examples of questions you can ask are:

- How do I act under pressure?
- Am I fair in my treatment of others?
- Am I thoughtful?
- Do I communicate clearly?
- Am I a leader?
- Am I genuine?
- Do I do what I say I'll do?

These are just a handful of questions you can ask people to answer about you, but ultimately it's up to you to decide what characteristics you want people to evaluate. Think about the things that could help you succeed in your current situation. Are you excelling at all the things you need to do well? If not, do you know what you need to do to improve?

It's my experience that people don't know the things they're not good at, myself included. It took me a long time to develop a better understanding of who I am. Even with my improved self-awareness, it's important for me to communicate with those around me to make sure I'm doing all the things I need to do.

It's easy to get slightly off-track and find myself in a challenging spot.

The second technique I would use is to evaluate yourself from afar. You need to take a moment to step out of your body and assess yourself. When you first do this, you might even have to be overly critical in order to remove any potential bias you may have. One of the best ways I get myself in the right mindset to evaluate myself is to take the questions I want answered and first evaluate a peer. Answer the questions that you eventually want to answer for yourself and see how someone else ranks in your mind.

Using the same approach to evaluating your peers, answer your questions about yourself. Treat yourself as a peer. It will take some practice, but if you spend some time evaluating others, you can get a feel for how you would want to evaluate yourself. Once you begin to evaluate yourself, you can begin to isolate what you do well and what you need to improve on. Then you can create a plan for what you need to do next.

By fully understanding your strengths and weaknesses, you can develop a plan of improvement to attack your weaknesses. You will also find that you put yourself in more situations where you're confident in your ability to succeed. I know there are things I'm not good at, so until I improve those areas, I don't put myself in a situation where I have to utilize skills I haven't developed. This leads me to more consistent success.

Self-awareness is one of the most challenging skills to develop. As I mentioned before, we tend to not know what we don't know. We're often blind to our shortcomings and inflate our strengths. I don't think we do this on purpose, but it still tends to be a problem. If you really pay attention to the people who are at the top of their game, whether that is in sports, business, leadership, or whatever, they tend to have a higher level of self-awareness.

A perfect example of this is a conversation I recently had with my friend Jason. He was telling me that he admired my ability to put myself out there and figure it out as I go. We were talking about my podcast and how he never would have put himself out there until he felt sure he could do a good job. On the other hand, I tend to put myself out there and, whether or not I'm prepared, I believe I can figure it out as I go. He said it's a trait he admires about me.

I looked at him and thought, "I don't even think about that when I do things." It's just part of who I am at this point. I've always had this ability to put myself out there and try things, even if I thought I could fail. This moment reminded me that self-awareness can't fully be achieved without others to help you. I didn't think I was doing anything unique or different by putting myself out there in this way. Yet, for Jason, it was something he wanted to emulate.

It's important to take time to talk to people about what they like and dislike about you, what they believe to be your strengths and weaknesses. Without someone from the outside, you may never fully grasp who you are. You may have a solid understanding of yourself, but there will be little things, like putting yourself out there, that others see as a special trait and that you don't even know you have. I'm grateful for the friends I have and their willingness to put into me love, support, and criticism when needed. We need a team to understand who we are and to become fully self-aware.

"By becoming self-aware, you gain ownership of reality; in becoming real, you become the master of both inner and outer life." -Deepak Chopra

Self-awareness is paramount when it comes to putting ourselves in a position to continue to see personal growth. It gives us the ability to objectively look at our strengths and weaknesses, goals and daily performance without bias. Without it, we blindly believe we're on the right path. The development of self-awareness is one of the most difficult things to accomplish and simultaneously one of the most important traits you can have. This creates quite a predicament on our quest for greatness. Some of the best have great self-awareness, but most people don't know if they're not self-aware—so where do we start?

As I mentioned above, two of the ways to begin are by self-reflection and by asking trusted friends in your life to give you feedback. There are also a few other ways you can begin to develop your self-awareness, which include journaling, meditation or mindfulness, writing down your specific goals and evaluating your performance in pursuing them, personality or psychometric tests, and taking time to objectively look at yourself.

If you've never taken a strengths finder test before, take a moment now to go take one. A few tests you could try would be a SWOT Test (Strengths, Weaknesses, Opportunities, and Threats), EQ-i 2.0 (Emotional Intelligence Test), or Clifton Strengthsfinder. I would also include one personality test (*https://www.16personalities.com/free-personality-test* is one of my favorites). This will give you a first look at your personality and some of your strengths. Once you know some of these strengths, you can go to work on your areas of weakness. I recommend revisiting these tests periodically because as you change, so, too, will your strengths. It might be fun to track how you evolve over time as well.

Another area that I'm not great at, but starting to implement into my life, is meditation and mindfulness. These two skills will allow you to better be present in the moment and aware of what you're doing right now. This will also give you a better sense of how you react in situations. When something happens in your life and you feel like you're emotionally reacting or not present in that moment, take a second (if you're able) to take a few breaths and ground yourself. Then reflect on how you're reacting and ask, "Is this how I want to respond?"

Self-awareness is a never-ending journey. You must commit yourself to being honest with who you are and own the areas you need to improve. Once you become more aware of who you are, you'll find you become better suited to achieve the outcome you want in various situations. You will have more control of your life. You'll be able to learn more from situations. You'll find you become closer to the success you seek. Reflect inward and start developing your awareness today for the future you wish to achieve.

Action Steps:

These might be your most challenging action steps. If you do this right, it will reveal a lot about you and who you are in this moment. Don't let that deter you, because this is just a starting point if you don't like the information you get. You're going to do self-assessments, ask friends and colleagues about you, and reflect, but you must not take anything you are told personally. It will be hard to not snap back, but remember, they're telling you these things to make you better. It's up to you to apply that information and put it to good use.

Areas you should invest time in to discover some extra self-awareness:
- Take a few tests:
  - Personality test/quiz
  - Self-awareness test/quiz
  - Strengths test/quiz
- Reflection
- Meditation/mindfulness
- Yoga/grounding techniques
- Journaling
- Observe others
- Ask for feedback (friends, colleagues, coaches, family)

As you can see, there is a lot that goes into becoming more self-aware. Don't try to solve all your problems at once. Attack a few things at a time. Take a few quizzes from different companies or sites and compare the results. Understand a little more about why you act a certain way in different situations, then slowly add in some more time getting to know yourself better. It will take time, but once you understand who you are, you will find an ability to achieve success in various settings.

"Self-awareness is a key to self-mastery."
-Gretchen Rubin

-Confident Enough to Believe Against All Odds-

"If you don't believe in yourself, no one will do it for you." -Kobe Bryant

Your success depends on being confident and pushing that confidence into the world. I understand it's not always that easy. Confidence has a tendency to come and go. There are days when you feel unstoppable and there are days when you don't believe you can do anything right. What I've discovered is, if you take time to master your mind and the way you think, you can be confident no matter what the situation. It is our mind that tells us we're not prepared or in a slump or not good enough. The mind is what the greats learn to control to give them the ability to display consistent confidence.

When I was coaching at Pickerington Central, I saw confidence show up and elevate performances, and I saw it disappear and destroy players who were once doing great. At the high school level these peaks and valleys are more prevalent, as these young men and women haven't spent as much time learning to control their minds. As coaches, it is one of our jobs to help them get out of their own way, to keep them from falling into the trap of thinking they can't. Once the mind says you're struggling, it's a lot harder to come out of the hole you dug.

During my first season with the softball team, I was throwing batting practice about three-quarters of the way through the season. We had been having some good success, but one of my players, Cami Fisk, had had a rough game recently. During practice, I could see her body language starting to deteriorate, and with it, her confidence in her hitting evaporated. She was feeling down on herself, and her confidence in her hitting was waning despite being in the middle of our lineup, where we put our best hitters, and batting well over .350.

Halfway through her second time hitting on the field, I stopped her round. I asked her what was going on, and I remember her saying something along the lines of, "I can't hit." I nodded my head as I listened, thinking about whether or not I should spew out the various stats or attributes she possessed, but decided to take a different route. She finished bashing herself, and I looked at her and said, "You know, it's hard to be a good hitter when you're so hard on yourself. Do you trust me?"

Cami nodded her head. I proceeded to remove the bucket hat I was wearing and put it on her head. I told her I wanted her to double knot her left shoe, pull out her right back pocket, and put my sunglasses on upside-down. She was laughing by this point. Then I told her she needed to bat left-handed for the next five pitches. To Cami's credit, she didn't argue with any of these requests, just turned around to the other side of the plate and proceeded to bat left-handed. For those of you reading this thinking it sounds familiar, I suggest you watch *Tin Cup* with Kevin Costner.

Cami stood in the left-handed batter's box looking about as goofy as anyone has ever looked on a softball field and proceeded to hit five line drives left-handed. Pretty good hits, actually. I peered from around the L-screen and smiled. "Looks like you can hit just fine to me," I said. I instructed her to flip around to the other batter's box again. She asked if she could take off the ridiculous costume, and I told her absolutely not.

I continued to pitch, and Cami blasted the first pitch into the left center gap off the fence. Then another line drive up the middle and a home run to left field. A few more missiles later, I stopped and came back around from behind the L-screen. I looked at her again and said, "Do you still think you can't hit?"

Cami smiled, "No, Coach."

"What do you think changed?" I asked. Cami shrugged, looking at me for answers. I smiled. "All I did was get your head out of the way. By making you look silly and bat from the other side of the plate, I stopped your brain from telling you that you can't do something and allowed you to focus on just making contact. Your brain was more occupied with how you looked and how silly it felt to bat left-handed that you let go of the negative thoughts you were having about your game. You're too good to let your brain tell you that you don't have what it takes. Tell yourself positive things or stop listening."

Cami smiled again. "Thanks, Coach," she said, then ran back into the dugout to get her glove and take the field.

After that day, everyone who was struggling with confidence would take a round of batting practice from the other side of the plate before batting on their normal side. It was an amazing moment for Cami and her teammates as they got a chance to see how powerful their minds were when it came to controlling their confidence and performance.

There will be times when confidence isn't high. We all go through moments like this. Sometimes it is because we know we didn't prepare for the moment. Sometimes it's because we don't believe in our abilities. Sometimes it shows up out of nowhere for irrational reasons. No matter why it shows up, we have the ability to counter these feelings. By ensuring that we prepared fully and know our abilities, we can then direct our minds to more positive or non-related thoughts to give us the ability to just do the task in front of us. Don't allow your mind to join forces with negative thoughts, but instead use it as a weapon to fight off doubts and insecurities.

"Confidence is when you believe in yourself and your abilities, arrogance is when you think you are better than others and act accordingly." -Stewart Stafford

I've always believed in my abilities. This belief started as an athlete but now has spread into everything I choose to pursue: business, coaching, speaking, consulting, parenting. I believe I will be good at anything I choose to put my mind to. Not because I already possess the skills necessary to be successful now, but because whatever I lack I can learn, and nobody will outwork me. This confidence gives me strength to try new things, attempt difficult tasks, and brave the unknown. It's also incredible how the more things I'm willing to try, the more successful I become, and the more confidence I gain.

I've been betting on myself for as long as I can remember. During high school I attended a fall baseball academy with some of the best baseball players in the Columbus, Ohio, area. This fall academy was known for helping baseball players make it to the next level. They did skills development, played in tournaments, and tested you at the end, giving feedback on where they saw your skills translating to the next level. It was during the final evaluation period that I learned to never listen to those who tell you that you can't do something.

At the end of training, I received my evaluations. According to the staff, I was a DIII (NCAA Division 3) baseball player at best. Now, I'm not taking anything away from any level of college baseball—there are many DII and DIII programs that would wipe the floor with some lower-level DI programs—but I knew I was better than their evaluation. I believed in my abilities as an athlete and baseball player. Instead of accepting this evaluation and giving up on my dreams, I dug in more and worked harder. Eventually, as I mentioned before, I earned a scholarship to a DI institution and became an All-American.

The initial evaluation of my abilities hurt. I felt as if I had spent all this time and effort to become a good baseball player for nothing. It took me a few days before I looked at my abilities honestly. I compared what I had as far as skill and physical abilities compared to my peers and decided that if they were perceived as Division 1 prospects, I could be, too. I think this is an important part of the process of believing in yourself. You can't just ignore everyone and blindly believe. You have to be willing to expose your weaknesses. You have to look yourself in the mirror and tell yourself the hard truths. Then you have to take all the critical evaluations and ask where the truth is. Most people who evaluate you aren't out to sabotage your future. They're trying to give you constructive feedback about your current abilities and, while they're going to get some things wrong, they're going to be spot-on about other things.

You have to figure out where they're right and where they're wrong, all while maintaining confidence in your abilities. You may be behind currently. You may be smaller, slower, less athletic, or less skilled than your competitors, but that doesn't mean you can't improve. Be confident that you have what it takes to rise to the level of your competition and then beyond. Confidence doesn't mean you get a free pass on the work needed to win. It just means you believe you have it within you to eventually find success, and you know you'll never stop 'til you get there.

Be confident in your abilities. Be confident you have what it takes. Be confident that nobody can stop you. Be confident to the point where people consider you cocky. But be aware that your confidence should be aimed toward things you can back up. Your confidence should be in things you know you can do or know you will be able to do given time. Don't let your confidence turn into arrogance, because that's when you lose focus on doing the work. Confident people still put in the work. Truthfully, confident people probably put in more work than their peers. Arrogant people believe they're above the work, that they don't need to work anymore. Nobody can skip the work! Know the difference!

"A calm mind brings inner strength and self-confidence." -Dalai Lama

When you look at someone who is successful—a high-profile celebrity or athlete, a powerful leader—they all display incredible levels of confidence. This belief in themselves and their abilities allows them to take risks and try new things. They don't fear an outcome because they know they have what it takes to figure out any mistake or shortcoming. Even if they happen to fail the first time, their confidence in their abilities gives them an advantage and makes them more likely to stick to it.

Yet somehow, even with how apparent self-confidence is among high-level performers and leaders, we try to deter people from displaying their own self-confidence. We belittle those who display high levels of confidence, calling them cocky, arrogant, or claiming that they have a huge ego.

Did you know that if you Google "most confident athletes," the second search result is "The 50 Cockiest Athletes of All Time"? That's not what I searched for, but we lump confidence in with cocky. Why do we fear a confident person? Why do we make confidence out to be some trait only held by the hated or vilified? Also on page one of my Google search are a video about cocky athletes and an article about "10 Has-Been Athletes With The Biggest Egos." How often have you seen an athlete display confidence about a performance or an upcoming game and comments range from "way to be humble" to "cocky a-hole" and everything in between?

I believe this negative outlook toward confidence steers people away from displaying their confidence.

Why would you want to show your confidence if the world is going to perceive you as arrogant or cocky? Yet the people we look up to and admire all carry with them an extremely high level of confidence. So something has to give. We have to get past the idea of confidence being bad. We need to pursue confidence. I think being a little cocky isn't necessarily a bad thing, either.

I looked through the article of the 50 Cockiest Athletes and on the list are a handful of Hall of Fame performers. Names like Mike Tyson, Shawn White, Pele, Usain Bolt, Joe Namath, Kobe Bryant, Muhammad Ali, and Michael Jordan are just a handful that grace the list. When you look at just this small sample of "cocky" athletes, what do you notice? All of them were at one point during their careers considered the best in the world at their sport. Think about cockiness that presents itself in other fields besides athletics: coaches, entrepreneurs, and leaders. Who would you put on this list? Would they also be at the top of their field?

So, is cockiness bad? Do we see confidence as such a negative that we associate it with cockiness? Do we project a dislike for those who are successful so we just claim them to be cocky? I think there's a little truth in all of those questions. The truth is, however, those who achieve success have an extremely high level of confidence in their abilities. They believe they have what it takes to win in any situation. I think we all should adopt this belief in ourselves. We should stand tall in the face of any adversity we face, believing we have what it takes to succeed and achieve the results we seek.

I'm confident that I can do just about anything. Maybe not at first—obviously, if you asked me to fly a helicopter today, I'd fail—but because as I mentioned before whatever I lack I can learn, and I'm willing to put in the work. I don't believe anyone is necessarily special or gifted. Sure, people have advantages, but those who lack those advantages can overcome their shortcomings with work and confidence. If this weren't true, we wouldn't have outliers.

Some of you may have read that last paragraph and think I'm being arrogant. So let me clarify what I'm saying. First, I believe I'm capable of anything I put my mind to and decide to pursue, not that I'm going to succeed the first day I attempt a new skill. Secondly, I'm honest with myself that I will face obstacles and adversity. I'm honest with myself on my strengths and weaknesses in a given situation, and while I may not currently be prepared to succeed, I have the means at my disposal to achieve success. This is the biggest difference between confidence and arrogance. I don't have an inflated image of myself: I know who I am and know that I have flaws and obstacles to overcome. I also know that I will do the work necessary to be successful.

The greats don't lack humility when they are by themselves. In truth, they are probably more critical of their flaws than everyone else. They are constantly looking to improve and are never satisfied. However, they simultaneously believe they've put in enough work and effort to be successful now. It's this confidence, combined with an understanding that they need to constantly improve, that allows them to achieve extreme levels of success. When we look at that list above, all of these people were extremely confident in their abilities, but not one of them rested on those abilities. They all continuously looked for ways to improve. They weren't ignorant about their capabilities, they were honest. They knew they were good but also knew they could be better. There was no inflated belief in themselves, but honest trust in their skill and focus on improvement.

We need to stop fearing confidence. We need to start to carry ourselves with pride and use the power of confidence to succeed in life. The key to this is to stop worrying that other people will see your confidence as a negative. People who don't want to work hard and achieve their own success will always call you arrogant and cocky. That's part of the price of achieving greatness. People who don't want to pay that price will try to tear you down. Ignore them and remain convinced that you are powerful and capable. Stand tall in the face of negativity: usually this ridicule will come from people who aren't willing to pursue their own greatness and seek to tear you down.

"To be a champ you have to believe in yourself when no one else will." -Sugar Ray Robinson

Another reason confidence is so important for success is because you're not always going to show up feeling like you've got your best stuff. What I mean by this is that your performance level will vary day to day, week to week. Some days you'll show up and be unstoppable—everything you do is the best you've ever done it—and then some days you'll show up and can't figure out why nothing seems to be working. Nobody has their best day every day. It's not possible. Confidence allows you to compete with what you have on a given day. It removes the limitations that come with how you feel that day.

As an athlete, I had days when I'd show up and immediately know that every shot I took was going in, every pitch was going to hit its spot, and I was going to crush every pitch in the strike zone. Those were the easy days. Those days I was going to be unstoppable.

But those days were rare. They weren't the norm. It was nice when they showed up, but most of the time I felt good but knew I had to focus and dial it in. Then there were days when I'd show up and I didn't know if I was going to hit the rim, throw a single strike, or put a ball in play. It was in those days I leaned heavily on my confidence and competitiveness.

I'm not sure where I developed this ability or skill, but on days when I felt like I was competing with my C- or D-game, I shifted my mind to compete with different tools. I was confident that even when I was not feeling my best I could still beat you. I'm sure some of you read that and thought, "That's pretty cocky." Perhaps, but I knew I had put in enough time and effort to have various skills at my disposal and that even though something was off, I was going to find a way. My shot's off today, I'm driving to the hole and focusing on my ability to rebound and play defense. Struggling to find the strike zone with a certain pitch, I'm going to change my grip, arm slot, starting position for my windup, pitch sequence, until I figure out how to get the ball over the plate and let my defense go to work. Not swinging well, I'm going to lay down a bunt, work the count and be patient in my approach and just compete with you.

There's always a way to find and achieve success, but you have to have the confidence and willingness to take a chance and change your game or approach. You have to know you have done everything you need to do to be successful and believe in yourself. Too often I have seen players I played with or coached fall apart because they didn't show up with their A-game. They lacked the confidence in their abilities to find another way. Their confidence was linked to how they felt instead of being confident despite how they felt. Be confident no matter the situation, because as soon as you stop believing you can succeed, you've lost.

I still remember a basketball game from my sophomore year in high school. We were playing a rival school (Upper Arlington in Columbus, Ohio) at their gym. During warmups I felt off, missing more shots from the outside than I usually did. I'm not sure what it was—maybe it was the lighting, maybe my form was just a little off, or perhaps it was because I was just coming back from a sprained ankle—but no matter the reason, I knew my shot didn't feel great. While I sat at the end of the bench before the game was set to start, I remember running through scenarios from the game that was about to play out in front of me. I pictured myself driving to the hoop, locking down their leading scorer, and grabbing rebounds. I didn't waste time on shooting from the outside because I had decided I would play my game inside out this game.

I was a very physical guard. I liked contact, I played good defense, boxed out well and could jump well, so I was going to use my strengths that didn't require feeling good to do well. The game started out with me guarding the team's leading scorer (which was usually the case), and I got two steals in the first three possessions for easy layups. I continued to focus on my defense, shutting down their player, and on the offensive side, I continued to attack the rim without even thinking about outside shots.

At the half we had built up a fifteen-point lead. I had 4 steals, 12 points, 5 rebounds, and 4 assists. My lack of confidence in my shot had faded and I knew that I was going to have a great game. I didn't waste any time in the second half and we pushed our lead to more than twenty. I finished the game with 22 points, 14 rebounds, and 11 assists. I only really remember this game because it was one of the few triple-double games (double digit stats in three categories) in my high school career and it came on a day when I started the game not trusting my shot.

Had I not had confidence in my ability to do other things, I would have never had this game. Honestly, had I been like one of my friends who relied on their feelings to play well, I probably wouldn't have had success in this game at all. I had seen my friends completely fall apart in a game because they let their feelings and lack of confidence destroy their ability to compete before the game even started. There's always a way to win in every situation if you can remain confident in your ability to solve the problem at hand.

You're not always going to have your A-game. You won't always feel great going into a presentation or meeting. There are going to be days when nothing you do seems to work the way you want it to. On days like this, the person who is confident still has control over their performance. The confident person begins to look for new solutions and another way to compete and get the job done. They believe in their ability to win even when they're not performing well because they've put in the work and prepared for this moment. They understand there is a way around their shortcomings and struggles, and it starts with their confidence.

Action Steps:

Confidence is a tough one because nobody is going to give you confidence: you have to take it for yourself. Something that has helped me with my confidence over the years is removing myself from the result. Winning or losing doesn't affect my confidence in my ability. I want you to try to remove yourself from the results you achieve. Instead, tie your confidence to the preparation you make. Tie your confidence to the routine and processes you create and keep. What is your pre-game/meeting routine? What do you do that makes you feel prepared?

We often attach our confidence to our success, but that's an unfair assessment of our ability. Something I learned playing baseball is that you can do everything perfectly and still not succeed. This was a paramount revelation to maintaining confidence in defeat. Instead of basing confidence on results, it became about basing my confidence on my preparation and doing the best I could in a moment. If you are prepared and give your all, you should remain confident that you will get the result you want.

Instead of waiting for results to give you confidence, make your own confidence. Build your bulletproof confidence prep plan:

- Daily positive self-talk
- Create pre-game/pre-meeting routine
- Practice responding to negative outcomes
- Increase your knowledge
- Practice relentlessly

Take control of your confidence by knowing you're putting in the work necessary to be great. Tell yourself you've got what it takes. Be confident based on your effort, not the results. It may take time to achieve the success you want, but if you can find a way to remain confident in the face of adversity, success will eventually be yours. You have what it takes to be great. It's time to let yourself believe it.

"If you always put limits on everything you do, physical or anything else, it will spread into your work and into your life. There are no limits. There are only plateaus, and you must not stay there, you must go beyond them."
-Bruce Lee

-Compete Hard and Compete to Win-

"Believing that your competition is stronger and better than you pushes you to better yourselves." -Simon Sinek

In the words of Ricky Bobby, "If you're not first, you're last." Nobody remembers second place. Nobody should aim for second place when aiming for being great. Now, when your career is over and you look back on your journey to greatness, you can appreciate times you didn't win. But while you're in the process of becoming great, never settle for less than the best. Be motivated by the losses and push for more. Want to be first in everything you do. You may not always get there, but if you aim lower than first, you'll definitely fall short of first.

Throughout my career as a player and coach, I've had wins and losses, championships and losing seasons. I've made many memories over the years. It's funny how people always say you'll remember the times with your teammates, and part of that is true, but the stories I share the most are ones where we won. Times when we became champions. I talk about my college championship season more than I talk about my All-American year. Why? Because my personal success didn't make the team win. I may have had personal success during my All-American season, but the team didn't. The goal of team sports and competition is to win, not to personally succeed. Be competitive, chase greatness with everything you have, and want to win all the time.

I've always been competitive. I've wanted to compete with everything I ever did. From the early days of travel baseball and AAU basketball, I was someone who wanted to compete. I didn't shy away from the challenges that lay ahead of me. This competitive drive has fueled me through my college career and into my life as an adult. I don't do things just to do them, I do them to win. I'm not here just to play, I'm here to win. This can rub people the wrong way, but the truth is I don't care. If you don't like it, beat me. I believe me wanting to compete with you on everything is going to bring out the best in you. It's going to push you to be better.

I think that's why I loved Coach Gussler so much. He was such a great competitor. He was a winner and a fighter. He showed up every day and gave everything he had to the game of baseball and the teaching of young people. I still remember when I first got to high school and experienced my first fall ball season. Here was this coach toeing the rubber, preparing to pitch to a bunch of high school kids. He'd stand up on the mound striking out players and talking trash, smiling and loving the competition. We had some incredible moments against each other as he pitched against me during my four years of high school. We battled each other, and I believe his competitiveness brought out the best in me.

My favorite moment was during my senior year. At this point in my career, I was very confident in my abilities and knew I was a good player. Coach Gussler stood on the mound, talking shit at me the whole way to the plate. At this point in my career, though, he had also taught me how to ignore the noise, so it didn't bother me. Honestly, I couldn't even tell you what he said, I just know he was running his mouth. In my first at-bat he started me off with a knuckleball and laughed at me as I watched it go by. I took the next pitch and drove it into right field. When I got to first, I put my finger to my lips in a gesture used often in sports to quiet the crowd.

He looked at me. "Oh, it's like that. Get your butt back in the box."

I smiled and made my way back to home plate. I had no problem getting another at-bat. The first pitch came flying in toward my ribs as I spun out of the way. I remember throwing my hands up at him like, "What are you doing?"

He just stared back at me. "Get in the box!"

The at-bat lasted eleven pitches before I finally worked a walk. The outcome didn't matter, it was the fact that his competitive nature pushed me to want to compete with him to be better. In that moment, we forced each other to raise our level of performance, and I believe it inspired some of the younger kids there to see what it meant to fight for something: To be a part of our program means you're here to compete.

I'm competitive to a point that I pissed off my wife the day before our wedding at our rehearsal dinner. We had an amazing rehearsal dinner that was outside at a family friend's house. Amazing outdoor environment, incredible food, music, and games. One of these games was corn hole. Which is actually how I met my wife. I used to go to a local country music bar in Columbus every week and play corn hole. One night I was there playing corn hole and listening to country music, and this beautiful girl jumped up to play against my brother-in-law Rob and me. So, here we were, years after meeting playing corn hole, and I'm playing against my fiancée and the host of our rehearsal dinner. We were down a decent amount and it was my shot. Holed it. Holed it. Holed it. Holed it. Ballgame!

I was stoked. What a comeback! I was celebrating with Rob and then I saw Erin just glaring at me. Furious that we just beat her (she's just as competitive as me even though she'll say she's not), she stormed off, pissed, and I felt like that was the end of it.

A few years later, we were having a party at our house and we were playing corn hole again (she'd still never beaten me to this point). It was a close, back-and-forth game, and at the end of it my friend Shaun, who was on Erin's team, sank a shot to beat Rob and me.

As soon as the shot went in, my wife screamed from across the boards: "Ha! Suck it! Take that!"

I was annoyed we had lost, but also so confused as Erin walked toward me, closing the gap between the boards, talking smack and giving Shaun a high-five. It was at that moment I knew she is just as competitive as me, even though she tries to hide it. It was also at that moment I realized that without competition, we don't have big moments in life like this.

Now, I don't recommend competing with your loved ones like this all the time, but this was a rivalry that dated back to how we met. She knew what kind of person she was getting as a partner in life, and I knew I was getting someone to fight for everything with as well.

Again, I'm pushing for competition in everything because I believe it brings out the best in us. I believe we are hardwired to compete and strive for greatness. But we must also learn to compete through losses and hard times. There's a difference between losing and being a loser. Losing is part of competition, and it forces us to re-evaluate our position and make adjustments to improve next time. Losers make excuses, point fingers, blame everyone and everything but themselves, and become unbearable in defeat. You should hate losing and you should fight to win all the time, but you should also take losses as opportunities to learn and grow.

"Somehow, people act like I have no competition, but the thing is, the competition is so good that it forces me to be better than I even thought was possible." -Ronda Rousey

I want you to think about the greatest teams you've been a part of. Think sports teams, business teams, theater teams, band teams, math league teams, debate teams—it doesn't matter. What makes a team great? What team that you've been a part of do you talk about most?

There are two teams that I regularly talk about when I think back on my playing career in baseball. The first is my high school legion team that won the district championship and made it to the state tournament. The other is my 2004 college team that won the conference championship and went on to play in the NCAA tournament against Texas.

I played a lot of baseball during my life, with a lot of good teams and a lot of great teammates, yet I find myself consistently talking about these two teams more than any other. Outside of these two teams, I tell stories about my "old-man" volleyball team that went to Orlando and won a national championship. A recreational national championship gets more attention than three years of college baseball. A recreational national championship gets more attention than my freshman year of college, where I had my best year ever individually and was an All-American. Championship teams hold a higher standard in my mind than other teams no matter how close we were or how much fun we had or any other thing that team provided.

Why? Because the reason we compete in sports is to win! Winning matters. My greatest memories of playing sports are of championship moments and winning big games. I'd bet money that for anyone reading this, it's probably the same for you. The stories I cherish most from my time with great teams are of when we won. We're designed to compete for victory, but for some reason we started to care more about everyone's feelings than competing to win.

I believe this design to compete stems from a time when only the strong survived and living was a competition. It used to be that if you didn't win, you died. If you didn't compete for food you starved, if you didn't compete against neighboring tribes you were conquered, if you didn't compete every day for everything, you died. Obviously, the stakes aren't as high anymore: you can lose and still survive. I believe that desire to compete is still within us, however, and that desire to win still drives us. We must learn to harness this power and use it to improve daily and reach for greater achievements.

Another thing that lives within this desire to compete is a relationship with adversity. When we connect more deeply with competition, we open ourselves up to face potential adversity. Through this adversity, we become stronger. This is why we must compete. We must create competition whenever we can, we must embrace the adversity that comes from it, and we must grow and learn from every opportunity. The world needs the strong to survive still, and we don't become strong by avoiding competition and shying away from adversity.

We need to stop acting like kids don't know the score when playing in a league that doesn't keep score. There has never been a moment in my sporting career when I didn't know where I stood in a competition, even without looking at a scoreboard. Besides that, we should be keeping score in everything we do. Keeping score gives us feedback on where we need to focus our attention to improve. If you don't know what your score is, how will you know where to put your energy to get better?

The score is our assessment tool that tells us whether we're doing a good job or not. When we lose, there is usually a reason. The score can also include specific statistics within the overall score. For example, in baseball (a sport that loves to keep track of every stat possible), did we strike out too much, did we make too many errors, did we look at too many good pitches and swing at bad pitches, did we fail to get a bunt down or steal a base? All of these stats and questions play a part in whether or not we end up winning. Without keeping score, without paying attention to the details of each statistic, we don't know where to focus our energy during our next practice.

We should be striving to win every time there is someone in direct competition with us. We should be trying to win when we compete against our past performances. Winning matters. However, without statistics and scorecards, we don't know if we're making any improvements. Find out what scores matter in the areas you're pursuing and start tracking. Then, find out what statistics affect those scores and how your performance measures up. Track as much as you can as often as you can. Become obsessed with getting better and pursuing victories.

Now, I want to make sure I address that this doesn't mean we have to go out and cheat or be poor sports or develop poor social habits doing this. When you learn to compete the right way, you become a more successful person. You push yourself to be the best you can be in each moment, and when you fall short and lose, you learn from it so that next time you can be victorious. This competitive drive pushes us to learn from our losses. It forces us to become better in each moment and challenge ourselves.

Do you ever wonder why you perform better in games than at practice? Why you have more energy when you face an opponent than when you compete against yourself? Because we don't keep score in practice. There's no real chance of losing to yourself. There's no fear of losing or drive to win, so we don't give the same level of effort. The chance we could lose provides us with a boost of energy and a higher level of focus than at practice. Competition brings out the best in us. We rise to the level of our competition with increased energy and focus. We should seek competition every chance we get, and we should want to win everything we're involved in.

When you seek wins and competition, you create a competitive advantage for yourself. The world we live in today is so obsessed with not hurting feelings or lowering people's self-esteem that we've lost our competitiveness. If you choose to be different, if you choose to compete and win, your potential for greatness will increase versus your competition. Again, let me be clear: I'm not encouraging foul play or unethical behavior in order to win. What I'm pushing for is a world in which everyone pushes those around them to be better by increasing their effort and drive to want to win. Stop being satisfied with the "I lost, but at least I tried" mentality.

I think a lot of people shy away from becoming ultra-competitive because they're afraid of being viewed as a poor sport or sore loser. I think there are definitely people who don't handle losing productively. This is the thing about those who succeed at the highest level: It's not that they never lose but that they never let a loss deter them from their next win. By accepting that this moment has ended and you lost, you can move past it. Too many people want to argue the result of something as if they're going to change the outcome.

The moment is over. You win or lose, then you move on. This ability to compete with all you have in a moment and then accept the outcome is critical to consistent growth. Now, when I say "accept," I don't mean you have to feel good about losing or be OK with finishing second. You just have to understand that this outcome is finalized and the only thing you can control now is the next one. Once you embrace this, you can compete fully in each moment, own whatever outcome happens, apply what you need to in order to win next time, and continue to compete without hatred or ill will toward your opponent. Being an elite competitor and wanting to win doesn't mean breaking the rules or sacrificing relationships for wins. There is a balance, and each person must find the one that makes them their best.

"I play to win, whether during practice or a real game. And I will not let anything get in the way of me and my competitive enthusiasm to win." -Michael Jordan

When did "competition" become such a bad word? Why do we shy away from competing today? The world is pushing for everyone feeling good about their effort, and in the process, we've diminished the level of competition. We don't fight to win anymore, we just play for fun. We're satisfied with second place. Second place isn't winning. And in order to achieve greatness you have to win, you have to compete, you have to drive up the level of your play to defeat an opponent. Some of you reading this might be turned off by this, but the truth is, anything you choose to do in life is going to be a competition. If you apply for a job, you're competing with all the other applicants. If you're fighting for an agent, you're competing with everyone else who needs an agent. If you're looking for a scholarship, you have to beat out everyone else looking for that scholarship. Someone is going to come out on top, and someone is going to lose.

The thing about competition that I love the most is it forces people to rise to the occasion. Competition is like adding jet fuel to a fire. Sure, it can be a little volatile, but the end results are explosive. Let's look at some of the great rivalries throughout history that forced greatness: Coke versus Pepsi, Apple versus Samsung, Ford versus General Motors, UPS versus FedEx, Marvel versus DC. Each of these rivalries and competitions led to innovation and change that inspired a new generation of greatness. Without someone at the opposite end pushing against them, would these entities have continued to push to new levels of excellence?

Some of you may have looked through that list and thought, "Those are companies. Of course they are competing with each other." Well, here's another list for you: Peyton Manning vs. Tom Brady, Chris Evert vs. Martina Navratilova, Magic Johnson vs. Larry Bird, Tiger Woods vs. Phil Mickelson, Muhammad Ali vs. Joe Frazier, Nancy Kerrigan vs. Tonya Harding. Now, while the rivalry between Kerrigan and Harding took them to higher levels of performance, this would be an example of competition gone too far.

Without the competition that existed between these athletes, would they have pushed themselves to the level that they did? I believe it was because they had a competitor that challenged them to stay sharp and be ready that these greats pushed further and harder. They knew their rivalry would be on display again soon and didn't want to face the music if they showed up unprepared. It inspired them to continue to do more and be more.

Each of the aforementioned rivalries inspired greatness to emerge. Whether it was through athletic development or innovation, change occurred through competition. The chance of failure or loss forced another level of performance or focus. Without competition, we become comfortable with our place and we stop pushing toward future growth. We become stagnant in our approach to greatness.

I think this was part of my downfall in my playing career. I had too much success early on and there was no fear of losing my place, which led me to get comfortable. This comfort made me feel OK with cutting corners and working less. Compare this to my freshman year when I was out to prove myself and was competing with everyone. I was trying to earn my place. The competition made me raise my game.

There's another thing that happens when we compete and have a winner and a loser: We up our performance level. Like having a rival, the risk of losing forces a greater level of focus and effort. I'm so tired of us removing winning and losing from everything. The "everyone wins and gets a trophy" mentality just means nobody wins. We've lost our competitive drive, and those who can find it will succeed in life. While we may be able to control winning and losing for our children, eventually they'll have to face winning or losing in the real world, and that is much harsher. I'd rather we learn to win and compete from an early age. I won't let my kids and nephews win; they must earn that.

I was on Facebook the other day and there was a comment about winning silver at the Olympics. You don't win silver; you lose the gold and get silver. There's no person who goes into a competition at that level and says, "I'm shooting for second." The minute you're not competing to be your best, you'll find yourself completely out of the race. Compete to win. Losing is part of every great journey and it's not the end—unless you make it the end. True greatness comes from continuing to compete until you find yourself on top of the podium, leaderboard, standings, or wherever else winners are recognized. Real winners, real competitors aren't happy or satisfied with second. They want to be first.

The real world doesn't care how hard you tried. The real world isn't going to reward you for a close loss. The real world wants to see you compete. The real world wants to see you win. This is going to require you to work harder than everyone else, compete every day, and to win. This is going to require more than just showing up. It's time to start competing against everyone, including yourself. It's time to collect daily wins and watch how they add up over time. It's time to be different.

Action Steps:

The first step to being a better competitor is to stop making excuses for losses. Competitors don't make excuses for things; they learn and overcome the failures. Compete to win every time you have the chance, and own the result. You'll win some and you'll lose some, but no matter the situation, you have to show up ready to compete. There can only be one winner, and that is going to be you. Sure, you may not win at every opportunity, but your competitive drive will allow you to win the long game.

Secondly, if you want to become a competitor, you have to be willing to keep score. You have to know if you're winning or losing. Being a competitor doesn't mean you win at all costs. It doesn't mean we cheat or cut corners for the win. True competitors compete within the rules and accept the results. It doesn't mean we become vindictive or poor winners/losers. We keep score to know whether the work we're putting in is paying off. We keep score to know where we stand in a particular moment. We keep score so we know what we need to improve upon to succeed now and into the future.

"So many times people are afraid of competition, when it should bring out the best in us. We all have talents and abilities, so why

be intimidated by other people's skills?" -Lou Holtz

-Live to Higher Standards-

"You must own everything in your world. There is no one else to blame." -Jocko Willink

I think this chapter sets the tone for all great individuals and leaders. It's the standards we set for ourselves that keep us accountable to the path to excellence. The greats find a way to uphold those standards every second of every day. They don't allow themselves to cut corners or slip. They do the work, they stay the path, and they commit themselves to doing things right every day, no matter how they feel. This is the path to excellence: doing the little things well each and every day and not accepting less than the best from yourself even when you don't feel like giving it.

I'm going to start you with a story about 17 inches. I've heard it numerous times over the years, and I feel it deserves a place in this book. It's the story of a speech given by John Scolinos during an American Baseball Coaches Association conference in 1996.

In 1996, Coach Scolinos was 78 years old and five years retired from a college coaching career that began in 1948. He shuffled to the stage to an impressive standing ovation, wearing dark polyester pants, a light blue shirt, and a string around his neck from which home plate hung—a full-sized, stark-white home plate.

After speaking for twenty-five minutes, not once mentioning the prop hanging around his neck, Coach Scolinos appeared to notice the snickering among some of the coaches. Even those who knew Coach Scolinos had to wonder exactly where he was going with this, or if he had simply forgotten about home plate since he'd gotten onstage. Then, finally…

"You're probably all wondering why I'm wearing home plate around my neck," he said, his voice growing irascible. The room laughed, acknowledging the possibility. "I may be old, but I'm not crazy. The reason I stand before you today is to share with you baseball people what I've learned in my life, what I've learned about home plate in my 78 years."

Several hands went up when Scolinos asked how many Little League coaches were in the room. "Do you know how wide home plate is in Little League?"

After a pause, someone offered, "Seventeen inches?" It sounded like more of a question than an answer.

"That's right," he said. "How about in Babe Ruth's day? Any Babe Ruth coaches in the house?" Another long pause.

"Seventeen inches?" A guess from another reluctant coach.

"That's right," said Scolinos. "Now, how many high school coaches do we have in the room?" Hundreds of hands shot up as the pattern began to appear. "How wide is home plate in high school baseball?"

"Seventeen inches," they said, sounding more confident.

"You're right!" Scolinos barked. "And you college coaches, how wide is home plate in college?"

"Seventeen inches!" the crowd yelled in unison.

"Any minor league coaches here? How wide is home plate in pro ball?"

"Seventeen inches!" The coaches shouted at the stage.

"RIGHT! And in the major leagues, how wide is home plate in the major leagues?"

"Seventeen inches!"

"SEV-EN-TEEN INCHES!" he confirmed, his voice bellowing off the walls. "And what do they do with a big-league pitcher who can't throw the ball over seventeen inches?" He paused, scanning the crowd. "They send him to Pocatello!" he hollered, drawing raucous laughter.

"What they don't do is this: They don't say, 'Ah, that's OK, Jimmy. If you can't hit a seventeen-inch target? We'll make it eighteen inches or nineteen inches. We'll make it twenty inches so you have a better chance of hitting it. If you can't hit that, let us know so we can make it wider still, say, twenty-five inches.'"

He paused again, letting his message sink in. "Coaches, what do we do when your best player shows up late to practice? Or when our team rules forbid facial hair and a guy shows up unshaven? What if he gets caught drinking? Do we hold him accountable? Or do we change the rules to fit him? Do we widen home plate?"

The chuckles gradually faded as four thousand coaches grew quiet, the fog lifting as the old coach's message began to unfold. He turned the plate toward himself and, using a Sharpie, began to draw something. When he turned the plate toward the crowd, point up, a house was revealed, complete with a freshly drawn door and two windows.

"This is the problem in our homes today. With our marriages, with the way we parent our kids. With our discipline," he said. "We don't teach accountability to our kids, and there is no consequence for failing to meet standards. We just widen the plate!"

Another pause. He turned the plate back to himself, and to the point at the top of the house he added a small American flag. "This is the problem in our schools today. The quality of our education is going downhill fast and teachers have been stripped of the tools they need to be successful, and to educate and discipline our young people. We are allowing others to widen home plate! Where is that getting us?"

His eyes surveyed the room as the crowd held their breath. He replaced the flag with a cross. "And this is the problem in the Church, where powerful people in positions of authority have taken advantage of young children, only to have such an atrocity swept under the rug for years. Our church leaders are widening home plate for themselves! And we allow it."

"And the same is true with our government. Our so-called representatives make rules for us that don't apply to themselves. They take bribes from lobbyists and foreign countries. They no longer serve us. And we allow them to widen home plate! We see our country falling into a dark abyss while we just watch."

"If I am lucky," Coach Scolinos concluded, "you will remember one thing from this old coach today. It is this: If we fail to hold ourselves to a higher standard—a standard of what we know to be right—if we fail to hold our spouses and our children to the same standards, if we are unwilling or unable to provide a consequence when they do not meet the standard, and if our schools and churches and our government fail to hold themselves accountable to those they serve, there is but one thing to look forward to…"

With that, he held home plate in front of his chest, turned it around, and revealed its dark black back side: "We have dark days ahead."

His message was clear: "Coaches, keep your players—no matter how good they are—your own children, your churches, your government, and most of all, keep yourself at seventeen inches. Don't widen the plate."

Coach Scolinos died in 2009 at the age of 91, but not before touching the lives of hundreds of players and coaches.

"Refuse to lower your standards to accommodate those who refuse to raise theirs." -Mandy Hale

This is an incredible story of accountability and why the standards we keep affect everything. Greats understand that they must live to a consistently higher standard than everyone else if they want to stay on top. This standard keeps them putting in work when they don't feel like it, doing things right when nobody's watching, and consistently expecting more from themselves instead of settling for good enough. I believe something that separates a high achiever from the average person is this understanding that standards matter and how we do things is vital to our success.

The truth about pursuing something at a high level is you're going to have days when you don't feel like doing the work. You're going to want a break. You won't have your best stuff, or you're just tired. On those days, what do you choose to do? Do you give in to the feelings you're having or do you find a way to show up anyway to get the work done? You're not going to feel good every day, or feel motivated and ready to work. These are the days that the best create space between themselves and everyone else. When others give in to these feelings and hit the snooze, skip a workout, or do less, greats show up and get it done.

There's something powerful about getting work done when you don't want to. Honestly, I think by pushing through those feelings and getting to work we sometimes create the environment to have our best days. As a college athlete I had many days where I didn't want to get up to go lift, or go to practice after a long day of class, or get my extra work in because I had assignments to do. Yet, those seemed to be days where I got my best work done. I focused better at practice, I lifted stronger, and I was more efficient with my extra work.

As a new father, business owner, trainer, coach, podcaster, and writer, I find my time slipping away from me on a consistent basis. I often have workout time set aside, but when that time comes, I feel like taking a break instead of lifting. But that time is already set aside for workouts; that's not my rest time. So I grit my teeth and get the ball rolling. The first few warmup movements hurt and are sluggish, but I just keep moving. Then, before I know what happened, I'm into my workout and crushing it. I feel strong and ready to get my work done, and after the workout I'm refreshed and motivated to take on the rest of my day.

See, we can't rely on motivation to get things done for us. We must rely on our standards of excellence. We must set expectations for ourselves and not "widen the plate" when things don't feel good. Instead, we must lean into our accountability structures and get work done on the days that are hardest for us to do so. It's the hard days when we make the most progress. This is the time when we gain ground on our competitors or separate ourselves from our challengers. Next time you don't feel like it, what will you do? Will you make an excuse for yourself and "widen the plate," or will you hold yourself accountable to the standard of excellence you expect from yourself? Choose wisely.

One of my favorite stories of a high standard of excellence is that of Steph Curry. I first heard this story in a speech given by Alan Stein Jr. Anyone who's been around sports has probably heard this story by now, but I'm going to share it again. The story is one of perfection, something that is very hard to achieve. Steph Curry refused to leave practice until he swished ten consecutive free throws. For those of you who don't know, a "swish" is a ball that passes through the hoop without touching any of the rim. He would stay as long as it took to make ten in a row.

I remember hearing a story of a time when someone was watching Steph after practice. He was shooting his free throws as usual and didn't know anyone was watching. He had made nine consecutive swishes before the tenth shot went in, nicking the back of the rim. He could have called it a night, he could have been happy with the make, could have said, "That's good enough." Instead, he grabbed the ball, returned to the free-throw line, and started over. Steph didn't have to do this. He didn't have to make ten swishes after every practice, but he set the standard and lived it. He will now be considered one of the best shooters to ever play the game of basketball.

If we look at this example of excellence compared to the world today, we discover a huge discrepancy. We too often are giving excuses or allowing for corners to be cut. In schools, teachers give extensions on projects, create curves, or give extra work for kids to make up missed points. We think by doing this we're helping our young people get good grades and pass classes, but what we're doing is lowering our standards. We're widening the plate. We're giving our youth the mindset that says, "If I don't do what's asked of me now, I can do something else later."

Take a minute and look at your life. Have you ever said you're going to do something and didn't? Have you ever committed to completing something and then cut corners or took the easy way out? Have you skipped reps or sets in a workout or done a "good enough" job and settled? Has anyone you lead or coach ever broken a team rule and you gave them a lesser punishment or no punishment at all? How many times have you set a standard and changed it when it got hard?

If you don't like the answer to those questions, it's OK. You're human like everyone else, and we all fall short of our standards at some point. I'd bet even Steph Curry has had a moment of weakness (maybe not when it comes to basketball, but somewhere). It's hard to always hold yourself accountable and to live life to high standards of excellence. I have had moments where I've been very good about holding myself accountable and other times when I have settled for "good enough." It's a constant battle, but if we commit to wanting more than just being good, if we commit to being great and understand that the standard to be great doesn't allow for these mistakes, I believe we can do better. I believe we can become more consistent.

This is one of the most important attributes of being great. I also believe this is one of the more challenging ones because only you know if you're cutting corners. Nobody is holding your hand or telling you when you failed a standard. No one is going to call you out on skipped reps or sets. No one is going to know what standards are expected of you, except for you!

We all have moments of weakness. We all struggle with not wanting to do something. But if you believe the thing you're doing is going to help you achieve the success you desire, do it to the standard you've set. You may not be happy doing it in the moment, but you'll be happy with the end result when the dust finally settles.

Action Steps:

Today you stop making excuses for cutting corners. You set the standards of excellence you want to live by and you don't allow yourself to do less. It starts with setting rules for yourself. You must have rules that you choose to follow and rules that those you let in your life must follow. If you're a leader, you will also have to set rules your team must follow. Once you set the rules, there are no exceptions, so make sure you're deliberate in deciding what to do.

Each day you must assess whether you lived your standards. You must own any mistakes or missteps that may happen. You're not going to be perfect—that's not what this is about. But you will be honest about how you live your life. You will own moments in which you make a mistake. Then, over time, you will find that you take fewer wrong steps. You will find that it's easier to uphold your specific standards. Be honest about what you're capable of doing, and live your life full of purpose and with high standards.

"You are never really playing an opponent. You are playing yourself, your own highest

standards, and when you reach your limits, that is real joy." -Arthur Ashe

-Goals: The Target for Your Journey to Success-

"If you aim at nothing, you will hit it every time." -Zig Ziglar

Goals are nothing without a plan. But just as bad is a plan without a goal. The two must be combined if you want to see progress toward becoming something more. There must be specific goals, a plan with checkpoints, and contingencies for when the plan goes wrong. All of these things working together give you a chance to succeed. If any part of this fails, there is a good chance you will find yourself off course and looking for a way to adjust the sails.

As I mentioned earlier in this book, one of my biggest dreams was to play college baseball. This had been a dream of mine since my first days of T-ball. Obviously, as a young player, I didn't have the greatest planning abilities, so I relied on being a hard worker. I knew that if I was going to be a college athlete I was going to have to work harder than everyone else. I started lifting at an earlier age than all of my friends, I went for runs, and I played sports every second of every day. My plan was basic, but I followed it closely.

As I got older, my plan became more detailed. I had a better understanding of what I needed to do and what I needed to work on. A lot of my plan still revolved around outworking everyone, but now I was more specific with my regimen. I worked out three to four times per week, I long-tossed two times per week, I hit two to three times per week, and I took ground balls one to two times per week. It didn't matter what else was going on. I always made time to do these activities.

As my skill and athleticism grew, I wanted to add a new part to the plan to give myself an advantage, so I added in watching baseball with a specific focus on learning tactics and approach at the plate. I studied different plays and why they threw to the different bases in various situations. I watched how pitchers attacked different batters, and I paid close attention to how the great hitters approached their at-bats. Each of these again moved the needle in the right direction for me to achieve my goal of playing in college.

When I got sick my junior year of high school, I was forced to implement a new plan. My current plan wasn't going to be enough. I had to make up for the lost time and setback of being sick. I revamped my plan, adding days and times to my workouts and study time. I became all about baseball every free moment of every day. I put aside relationships that didn't help me achieve my goal.

The plan worked and I made it to college. As I mentioned before, my freshman year I continued to operate with a strong and detailed strategy. I let success and distractions take me off course, however. I stopped creating a detailed blueprint for achieving my goals. I still had big goals, I still wrote them out and put them where I could see them, but my plan was nowhere to be found. My goal had become a wish. I was no longer changing course to match the winds, I was just floating where the current pushed me.

It wasn't until my senior year that I rededicated myself to the plan . Unfortunately, it was too late for me then. I finished up my career and moved on with my life into the real world. It took me a while to find my way again. I had various goals, but nothing that was a serious focus until I became a gym owner and coach. It was getting back into baseball and working with athletes that ignited my passion for helping others. I'm now following a new plan—this book is part of that plan. I'll let you know how it works out.

"If you don't know where you are going, you will probably end up somewhere else." -Lawrence J. Peter

Goals are the Waze app on your journey to success. Without goals, we have no end point to create directions from. Just like Waze offers multiple routes to our final destination, we, too, must decide which path we're going to take in life to achieve the goals we want. Sometimes we need to take the scenic route, sometimes we need to be more direct in our approach, but at the end of the day we need to trust the path we choose and keep making progress toward our destination. The other great thing about plugging our goals into the GPS of life is that when we get stuck or find ourselves in traffic or off course, it will recalculate and get us back on track.

Too often we go after things without creating a plan, thinking that is how goals work. Goals without a plan are a wish. Saying you want something without planning how to get there is a recipe for failure.

Creating the plan and preparing for obstacles and potential adversity are some of the most critical parts of goal-setting. How many times have you had a goal in your life without creating a plan? If you're anything like me, you probably had many goals growing up that you didn't have a single idea how to make happen. I think that's something everyone goes through before learning how to properly set goals.

As I mentioned earlier, a goal without a plan is a wish. Take a minute to think about the things you wanted to be growing up. How many of you have pursued a career aligned with those dreams and goals? Growing up, I went through a phase where I wanted to be a paleontologist. For those of you who don't know what that is, I wanted to study dinosaurs. I was obsessed with them. I asked my mom the other day what other careers or paths I wanted to take besides that growing up. She told me after that it was all sports all the time. I wanted to go pro in every sport there was.

I'm not sure if this is the case for everyone reading this book, but I do find it interesting that I was so singularly focused on sports and athletics. I remember wanting to be a pro baseball and basketball player growing up, but I was sure there had to be something else I was missing. According to my mom, who's always right, it was all about sports for me. It makes sense that I've traveled the path I have. Every rest stop, detour, new destination plugged into my GPS had something to do with sports and performance. There was always a plan for what to do next when it came to athletics; I had no plan for becoming a paleontologist.

I fully believe this is why I've always had a path to travel. I knew the directions to get to my destination. I had a goal and a plan. At times on my journey to where I am today, the road was an expressway to my next stop, and sometimes it was a dirt back road, but I was always making steps toward a career in athletics. I've been an athlete, coach, and trainer during this journey. My overarching goal has always been to make an impact in sports. As my playing career began to wind down, however, I've slightly adjusted this goal to be: I want to make an impact through sports. I want to use sports to teach life skills and develop better people and leaders.

My goal has not changed entirely, but the address has changed a little. I'm still heading to the same city, but the new address is in a different part of town. I think this is why having specific goals and plans is important. While you may not always achieve the goal you initially set out to achieve, the more specific your destination, the more likely you are to use that goal to inspire a new goal.

What I mean by that is we all evolve with time, and our goals will shift as we go through life. My initial goal was to become a professional baseball player, and while that is no longer my goal, it has inspired me to want to stay involved in sports. My goal now is to help others achieve the best version of themselves (usually this is in sports, but I coach all aspects of life). Without that initial specific goal, I wouldn't have achieved what I did in baseball, which opened up doors for a career in sports that didn't involve being a professional. Sometimes the shift is big and drastically different and in a whole new direction, and other times, like with me, it's a small and subtle shift. Either way, without a goal and target to shoot for, we wander aimlessly through life.

I've discovered that we perform better day-to-day with direction. Humans are designed to attack goals and dreams. We're designed to discover a sense of purpose and pursue it fully. Without purpose, we're lost. We lose our drive and find ourselves unhappy at our core. I think it's important to say that your purpose doesn't have to be a global kind of purpose. You don't have to want to be a superstar athlete, a world-class musician or a highly regarded author or speaker to make an impact on the world. It could be as simple as being the best parent or teacher you can be. It could be a purpose that doesn't impact anything outside of your community. This is all completely fine, but the important piece is having a purpose, having a reason you get out of bed and attack the day.

I know finding a purpose can be a challenging task. I also know that our purpose can change and evolve over time. Having a gauge on this purpose is critical. By understanding what drives you each day, you can better set goals and expectations for yourself and drive your daily activities. My purpose has evolved from being the best athlete I can be to being the best trainer to being the best coach and leader I can be. My life is now all about understanding high performance and how I can best help others achieve that. My purpose has changed, but I've rarely had moments in life where I didn't know my purpose. I've always tried to have a strong grasp on the direction I'm traveling, even if the destination wasn't fully in focus.

"Shoot for the moon. Even if you miss, you'll land among the stars." -Les Brown

While goals serve as a road map to where the future you wants to go, they should also be big enough to inspire you to pursue greatness. Too often, we set safe goals. We set goals we know we can achieve. They may be slightly beyond our current abilities, but well within reach. I believe we should be setting huge goals,

goals so big that it makes people question whether we may be reaching for too much. These are the goals that make champions emerge.

I'm not sure why I tend to see people setting safe goals, but it's definitely common. I had a conversation recently with one of my hitting clients about his goal to play college baseball. He told me he hadn't emailed any Division 1 teams about playing for them. His reasoning was that he didn't think he was what Division 1 teams were looking for. I think he could play at the Division 1 level, but he would definitely have to put in the work for it.

While I mentioned earlier the value of self-awareness, don't use your perceived limitations as an excuse to play it safe. Self-awareness is there for you to understand how much work you'll need to put in in order to achieve your goals. Don't let the standard deter you from pursuing a goal that may seem beyond your reach. There are always outliers—people too short or small, too slow, not as smart, from the poor part of town—who make it big. They didn't use their limitations as an excuse, but instead went to work on what it was going to take to be successful.

By setting big goals, you give yourself a target to aim for that's well beyond your current situation. It creates an internal motivation to pursue excellence every day in hopes of one day achieving this massive goal. By lining up a target that is so far out that you can barely see it, you wake up each day reaching for the stars. Even if you fail to ever achieve that goal, you'll be so much further ahead than if you had set a goal so close you could already touch it. Be bold in your goal-setting. Set massive goals, then each day take a small step toward achieving that goal.

Another piece of creating success is finding appropriate checkpoints to celebrate along the way. If your goal is so big that you know you won't get there anytime soon, then you have to find moments and points along the way to celebrate your progress. Without these checkpoints, it's easy to get lost in the day-to-day and lose hope that you'll ever achieve your dream.

Each small victory on the path to your bigger goal adds momentum to your journey. Celebrate that victory—but only for a moment—then get back to work. Set a clear plan of what it will take for you to make your dream come true. Once you have that clear plan, mark the various checkpoints along the journey. Each time you reach a milestone, appreciate what you've done, then re-evaluate your plan to make sure the course you have set still is the best route.

It's OK to recalculate your route if a better path presents itself. Don't get so lost in the journey that you don't look to see where you are. The consistent re-evaluation of your plan and path allows you to stay on course. If we ignore the fact that circumstances and situations change along our way, we might find ourselves off course and wandering aimlessly through the sea of life.

One of my favorite stories about goal-setting and course correcting comes from James Clear, the author of the bestselling book Atomic Habits. Imagine you're taking a flight from Los Angeles to New York City. It's always been your dream to visit the Big Apple, but at takeoff the pilot adjusts the plane 3.5 degrees to the south. At the time of take off, 3.5 degrees is seemingly insignificant. However, during the course of the flight, that 3.5 degrees leads the plane to eventually land in Washington, DC, instead of New York City. The plane at the time of landing is 228 miles off course.

While DC could be fun, and maybe you'll be OK with the final destination, it's not New York City. A seemingly insignificant adjustment at takeoff caused an entirely different final destination. The goals you set and the habits and plans you put in place to achieve that goal determine your ultimate destination. Another part of this story is that if we had checked our heading at some point during our trip, we could have slightly adjusted our heading and gotten back on course.

When you think about the journey to achieving your goals, I want you to think about sailing. During a sailing adventure or race, the participants have a course they're trying to navigate, but for the majority of the race they're actually going the wrong way. In order to catch the wind, the boat must turn and adjust regularly over and over again. The boat actually travels in a zigzag pattern throughout the entire race.

You will travel similarly on your path to achieving your goals. The majority of the time, you will probably appear to be off course. But as the winds change and you adjust your sails, you will find yourself inching closer and closer to your goals. Each turn to catch the wind is an attempt to make progress toward your goals, but if you were to just look at a single moment in the journey, it would appear you're going the wrong way. If you get a chance, go watch a sailing race and pay attention to how they constantly are adjusting their sails in order to reach the finish line. Don't be afraid to adjust your sails along the way.

Action Steps:

Go set one massive goal today. What do you want to achieve twenty years from now? Where do you want to be? Remember, this should be a huge goal that stretches you because we're not trying to get there tomorrow. We're trying to get there in twenty years. Once you have this goal, work backwards to determine checkpoints. Now that you have checkpoints, think about potential obstacles you may face along the way. Be real about these and how you plan to respond if one arises.

Goal-setting checklist:

- Set your main goal (twenty years or more into the future).
- Set checkpoints/milestones.
- List potential obstacles or setbacks you may face. This list may only include obstacles up to the first checkpoint.
- Revisit your main goal and checkpoints regularly. Remember to course-correct if you find yourself drifting.
- Make sure your goal and checkpoint plan are easily accessible.

Setting goals and creating a plan are vital to success. Just as important is knowing how you will attack potential setbacks and revising your plan throughout the trip. Just like on a long road trip, if you know there's an accident ahead, you may want to take a different route instead of sitting in traffic and waiting for it to clear out. It may feel like you're off course a lot, but as long as you have a plan and adjust it accordingly, you will find your way.

"The great danger for most of us lies not in setting our aim too high and falling short; but

in setting our aim too low, and achieving our mark." -Michelangelo

-Forged by Failure-

"Only those who dare to fail greatly can ever achieve greatly." -Robert F. Kennedy

An interesting thing about failure is how much we fear that word as a society and shame people for their failures. Greatness requires a payment of failure. I believe each of our failures is a test. It's a test of how important that particular pursuit is to us. On our journey to be great, failure is going to test our resolve. It's going to look at us and ask, "How important is this to you? How much are you willing to take?" Greatness is going to push us to our breaking point in attempts to make us quit. We will also spend more time with failure the closer we get to our goals and dreams. Ignore those who aim to bring you down for failing along the way: stay focused on what you know is possible. All you have to do is find the right path, and greatness is at the end of your journey.

I want you to think about where you are today. Think hard about each step, each turn, each obstacle that inevitably led you to where you currently are. Have you got a clear picture? Now think about some of the failures you've faced during this journey. Think about the times you came up short. Think about the moments you were pushed to the verge of quitting. Each failure in your journey is a milestone moment that forced you to make a choice, and that choice shaped you into who you are today. Whether in that moment of failure you chose to forge on or try something new, that moment became a milestone.

That might have been a lot to think about right now, and you might be wondering what I'm talking about. Let's start from the beginning, shall we? I'm going to tell you a story, and by the end you will understand how I became who I am today. You ready? This story starts from very early on in my life. Still unable to talk and weak in the knees, I started my journey of resilience and grit, facing my failures head-on. I was just nine months old and already I knew failure was part of the journey as I continued to try to put one foot in front of the other to make it across the room. Constantly falling and picking myself back up, each failure made me more determined to figure it out and make it happen. Imagine if, after the first time I fell, I decided it was too hard and quit? Imagine if, as a nine-month-old, I saw failure as an end result instead of part of the process. I'd still be crawling around, looking up at everyone else as they walked by.

As my journey in failure continued, I found myself faced with another opportunity to shape myself. At five years old, I was outside climbing a tree in my backyard. I really wanted to pick the pine cones off this one tree that stood in our yard. Not really sure why. Nevertheless, here I was toward the top of this tree, hanging off branches, reaching for pine cones to throw down to the ground. I was hanging when all of a sudden—*snap!*—the branch I was hanging on broke and I crashed to the earth. I bounced a couple of times, then ran into the house screaming (obviously a little scared). My mom checked me out, I calmed down, and she sent me back outside to play. I looked back at the tree and decided I would give it another go. So, back up into the tree I went. A few minutes passed and—*snap!*—tree branch broke and back to earth I fell.

Again I went screaming into the house. I don't remember what my mom told me or how she reacted to me falling out of the tree for a second time, but I do remember that I went back outside after calming down. Then, once again I climbed that tree, this time without falling, and finally picked the pine cones for my collection. Which I never saw again after that day.

Some of you may be reading this part and thinking, "He's just not very bright, is he?" Well, that may be the case, but I also learned that day that in order to achieve the things we want in this world, we must face our fears and overcome the obstacles that stand in our way.

I'm not sure why I wanted those pine cones, but I knew I wanted them. I also knew there was a chance that along my journey I could fall and potentially be hurt. But I didn't let the fear of falling, the fear of pain or failure stop me from pursuing what I wanted. I believe this is the day that I developed my stubborn resolve to work for what I want. I'm sure, had my mom stopped me from playing or kept me from ever climbing again because I fell, I may not be who I am today. I was forged by this moment, and I'm thankful for my failure—and for not breaking any bones in the process. That was good, too.

My life moved on and I continued to pursue athletic endeavors. I pushed myself to become the best athlete I could. I dreamed of being a professional athlete. Obviously, I was going to play in the NBA. In case you forgot, I'm five foot eleven and, while I can jump and shoot a little, the NBA for people five foot eleven or under is not likely. You probably can't name ten people six feet to play in the NBA.

Anyway, my freshman year I had just finished basketball season and baseball season was getting ready to start. Like I mentioned previously, I was set to be on the JV team as a freshman. But I wanted to play basketball, too, so I walked up to the coach and asked him if I could play AAU travel tournaments on the weekends as long as they didn't interfere with my baseball schedule. I told him I would never miss a game or practice and only play when we didn't have something for baseball.

He looked me square in the eyes and told me no. I begged and pleaded with him, but eventually gave up, having failed at persuading him to see it my way. I went home that night and told my parents I wanted to quit baseball, claiming the baseball coach didn't understand I could do both and that I was going to be a basketball player anyway. I failed to persuade them as well. I reluctantly returned to baseball the next week, knowing that I wouldn't be able to play AAU basketball, and committed myself to playing baseball. A week later I was moved up to varsity, and by the time the season started, I was the starting right fielder. I eventually became a four-year letter winner, a two-time All-Conference and District selection and became a

Division 1 collegiate baseball player (where I was a first team Freshman All-American).

Had I not failed at negotiating playing AAU with my coach and quitting baseball altogether with my parents, I may be a completely different person today. My failure led me to become a better baseball player, and playing for Coach Stephen Gussler, made me a better man. It also taught me that if I commit myself to one thing and really do my best, I can achieve great things. This was my greatest failure and without a doubt had the biggest impact on my future success. I'm so thankful for my parents encouraging me to stick it out and Coach Gussler telling me no. Even today, I carry his teachings and passion with me and try to instill it in the kids I work with.

In college I failed again. First, I failed in class—failing a couple classes during my freshman season as I learned to balance in-season travel and studying—and then I failed on the field. After being an All-American, I never really found my stride quite the same. I put most of that failure on the fact that I didn't work as hard as I did my freshman year, which we talked about earlier. But my greatest failure came when I was benched as a senior halfway through the year. I had started more than 150 games and found myself riding the bench. This was not a place I was used to being. It was hard for me to be there as I couldn't remember a time I had ever not played. Part of me wanted to quit and walk away because I didn't want to face my teammates or parents or anyone. I was crushed, and the worst part was, I never truly understood why I was benched for that long.

But I didn't quit, I didn't walk away. I kept showing up, I did what was asked of me. I cheered loud and played hard when I got opportunities. Then in the conference tournament I was given a chance to start again. I finished up the last two games of my college career as the starting shortstop. I also went 6 for 8 (six hits in eight at-bats) at the plate in the final two games. We lost and my career ended, but I didn't let adversity break me. I didn't let bad times stop me from pushing forward. In the end, I found a way to overcome everything and finish strong.

More recently I found myself as a coach for Pickerington Central softball. I joined a staff during great turmoil in the program and together the head coach, Jenny Young, and I righted the ship and began to produce great success. In two years we attained a district runner-up title and a conference championship, not to mention a pretty solid win percentage, only to find ourselves out of a job after two seasons. This was a pretty harsh blow, as I felt we were making great strides with this team and we were close to being truly special. Instead yet again I found myself on the failure train. This failure, however, led me down a new path, and I'm not sure I would have ended up where I am now without it.

All of these moments of failure on my quest to be the best athlete, coach, and leader I can be guided me toward starting a podcast to learn more about greatness. Had I achieved immediate success in any of these situations, I might not have developed the same resilience to adversity and probably would not have become as strong of a person. Failure sucks, and nobody enjoys failing. But when we shift the way we see failure, when we focus on the moment as a learning opportunity instead of a catastrophic event, we have a chance to use our failures to fuel our future successes.

"The difference between average people and achieving people is their perception of and response to failure."
-John C. Maxwell

Failure is a part of any great journey. The difference between those who achieve greatness and those who don't lies in how they perceive failure. The greats use it as a learning opportunity or fuel to power through their next obstacle, while the average person uses it to make excuses, quit, and blame. The reason why failure happens on great journeys is because during these quests we are wading into uncharted waters. To pursue excellence, we have to accomplish things we've never done before, and when we do that, we're bound to fail initially. I'm not sure why we assume we're going to find success so easily and not be tested, but I seem to constantly find people who want to complain about their failures instead of acknowledging them and growing from them.

When I think about what it takes to become successful in life, I think about the ability to learn from our failures and power on. I love using sports references, and I'm going to use another one now. If you haven't had a chance to watch competitive sport climbing, put down this book right now and go over to YouTube and check out bouldering. This sport is a perfect example of using failure for learning.

Each climber is faced with a problem they must solve within an amount of time. As you watch them study this wall and feel out different positions and holds, it resembles a person on a quest to discover or learn something new. They solve parts of the problem with ease, and then they find a part of the journey where they must pause to evaluate their next move.

Often in this moment of reflection, they make a move in an attempt to try and solve the problem and fail. They do this without fear of making a mistake but instead with the intention of discovering what could work. When they fall from the wall, they don't get angry or upset. They look back at the wall and play the move over again in their mind, working through the problem. Then they're back on the wall working their way up. They may fail several times along their journey to the top, but with each fall they get a little closer to solving the problem that lies ahead of them. It's an incredible visual of the learning process in action. Failure is just a part of the journey. The question is: what do you learn from that moment?

"I have not failed. I've just found 10,000 ways that won't work." -Thomas A. Edison

All great people fail. In fact, the great people, the most successful people, fail more than most. Legend has it that Thomas Edison failed 999 times before creating the light bulb. Imagine if he feared what people thought of his failures. Imagine if he didn't believe that each failure was a step along the journey to success. He's been known to say that he didn't fail 1,000 times, but that it took 1,000 steps to create the light bulb. Henry Ford failed and went broke five times before succeeding. Abraham Lincoln entered a war as a captain and returned as a private, then failed as a businessman. Winston Churchill repeated a grade during elementary school and twice failed the entrance exam to the Royal Military Academy. Reggie Jackson and Jim Thome have the most strikeouts in MLB history (2,597 and 2,548 respectively) but are both in the Hall of Fame. Nine out of the ten losingest pitchers in MLB history (250 losses or more) are also in the Hall of Fame.

I could go on, but I'm sure at this point it's become clear that failure is a great part of success. It's not just that we must fail, however, but that we must continue to pursue our dreams despite our failures. We must not become consumed by them or fear the next failure that may come. Instead, we continue to put ourselves out there. We walk that fine line between knowing we will succeed and knowing we will fail, and we live on the brink of our abilities, all while knowing there is a chance we may fail, and that's OK. If we choose to live this way, on the brink of success and failure, we may fall short at times, we may miss our mark, we may struggle and stumble along the way, but we may also make that next great breakthrough. We may find what we're meant to do and the true extent of our abilities. We may ourselves be great.

It's funny, though, that I used to think we should go looking for failure. I used to think that seeking out failure would lead us to success later, but during a conversation with Jon Gold (a mental performance coach), I found a new way of thinking about this. He doesn't believe we should seek failure because if we seek failure, we set ourselves up to fail. We shouldn't fear failure, but we should seek success with an open mind to learn from our failures. This is an important distinction, because in the pursuit of great things we're bound to face failure, but if we go into our pursuits looking to fail, we've set ourselves up to accept the failures before they happen. In a sense, we're giving ourselves an excuse not to succeed. We should strive to succeed and be great, but when failure presents itself—and it will—we must learn from that moment and adapt.

As you move on through life, I hope you remember that we are all forged by our failures. Each failure we face presents us with a choice. Do I continue to fight to accomplish that which I failed at or do I choose a different direction and a new path? The hard truth is, anything you truly love or have passion for you will fail at because when we are passionate and love something, we put ourselves out there further than we would otherwise. We try new ways of doing things, we challenge ourselves with more difficult opponents, we test our abilities.

Failure provides us with the test that we must pass in order to move on. We need to decide whether something truly matters to us. If what we fail at matters, we will double down and push on, but if it doesn't, we'll quit and choose a new path. Either way, that failure is driving our future self. My hope is that we choose to face our failures, that we embrace each moment we come up short and become stronger for it. Either way, remember that each failure is just a moment on the path to who we eventually become. We are all forged by failure.

Action Steps:

Your first action steps for this chapter are to rewind your life and do a deep dive into what has led you to where you are today. I want you to dissect your various quests and failures. I want you to think about how each failure changed you. Did you decide in that moment of failure to press on, or did that failure open up a new door for you? Once you realize that failures don't define your success, they just help direct your journey, you can attack each moment more freely without fear of failing.

After you discover that your journey to this point in your life is full of different failures, you will feel more free to take risks and try new things. Use that freedom to challenge yourself. I want you to take on a task or challenge you've been wanting to do for a while, but have been hesitant for fear of failure. This book is that for me.

Maybe you want to try a marathon or Spartan Race. Perhaps you want to start a blog or YouTube channel. Maybe you want to interview for a higher-level job. All of these come with a chance of failure, but each offers an opportunity to learn if you do fail. More importantly, you won't know what you're ready for if you don't take the first step. Be bold.

"Failure should be our teacher, not our undertaker. Failure is delay, not defeat. It is a temporary detour, not a dead end. Failure is something we can avoid only by saying nothing, doing nothing, and being nothing."
-Denis Waitley

-Sacrifice and Suffering are Part of the Journey to Greatness-

"You can only become great at that thing you're willing to sacrifice for." -Maya Angelou

I'm sure everyone who read this chapter title probably jumped out of their seat and yelled, "Yes, suffering and sacrifice. Let's go!" I mean, who doesn't like the idea of a little bit of suffering and discomfort in their life? Now, while without a doubt there are going to be moments of sacrifice and suffering on the journey to greatness, I'm not talking about offering up a lamb or being tortured. I'm talking about the choices we make to miss out on opportunities that don't align with our goals along with the work and discomfort we face by chasing our dreams.

When you think about all the things it is going to take to become great, there is no doubt you will have to make some difficult choices. You're going to have to choose to work late instead of going to the bar with friends. You're going to have to choose to get an extra workout in instead of playing video games. You're going to have to sacrifice time with family to make a sale or promote your new venture. There will be many sacrifices along the way, but the more you believe in your journey, the easier it becomes to make the hard choice. Greatness isn't going to just show up for you, you're going to have to make choices, and sometimes those choices will include doing what you have to do over doing what you want to do.

In high school I sacrificed a lot of my social standing and social life in the pursuit of becoming a college athlete. I'd choose to go work out or get extra work in over going to the movies or Friday night football games. I'd choose to go out of town for a tournament over partying with friends on the weekends. A lot of my choices and sacrifices were centered around this dream to be a college athlete. That was the important factor in helping me make these sacrifices because to me, they weren't sacrifices, they were just the right choices for my future. My friends felt like I was missing out on things, but I never felt that way.

On our journey to greatness, we are not the only ones who sacrifice. I still remember the time I got mad at my parents for planning a trip to California during basketball season. I didn't miss any games, but missing practice was more than I was willing to accept. I don't remember exactly how I acted, but I'm sure I was not fun to be around that week. I do remember driving to a local park each day for a few hours and practicing. I knew I wasn't able to get back home, but I wasn't going to miss out on my practice time. I still remember being furious (probably unfairly), and I'm so thankful I had parents who understood my dream of becoming a college athlete and never scheduled another trip during one of my seasons. They sacrificed family trips and vacations for my dream.

Sacrifice is going to be part of your journey. Whether you sacrifice personal time, family time, vacations, weekends off, sleep, a promotion, or any other number of things, sacrifice will be a part of your success. But if you have a vision of who or what you want to become, the choices become easier. I remember passing on an opportunity to play for our premier legion team during my sophomore summer. I was asked to play up with the older kids, and I knew I was capable of playing with them, but I also knew it wasn't the right fit for me at that moment. So I chose to play with my varsity summer team. The time playing "down" with them allowed me to develop into a leader, take on more responsibility within the team, and become confident in who I was on the ballfield.

I could have easily taken the opportunity to play with the better legion team, but I would have been just another number on that team. I wouldn't have been asked to be a leader. I wouldn't have been leaned on to be a captain. Ultimately, I don't think I would have developed the confidence I did playing with that team. Sure, I would have been challenged and it would have been a good developmental opportunity, but I used my time to develop other skills that I think added to my abilities as a player and led to a very good junior season.

The other part of this sacrifice is finding people you can surround yourself with who understand your sacrifices. In high school, that was my best friend Kyle, who never pushed me to go party, would shoot hoops and work out with me, and was always a fan of my efforts and performance. He had my back and was a constant motivator. Today, that person is my wife, who takes care of both of our kids so I can coach or go out of town for a conference. She takes on a lot for me to own my business and come home late. Her sacrifice allows me to pursue the success I seek.

Some of you reading this might be thinking that you don't have the ability to make these sacrifices. You can't take time off work to go to a conference that will help your future dreams. You can't take a weekend away from your family or do something late at night or early in the morning. Not to be harsh, but that is your choice. You're choosing to miss out on opportunities and not sacrifice. I had a conversation for my podcast with Jason Dutton (*The Edge of Greatness Podcast-* Episode 15 which can be found at www.theedgeofgreatnessproject.com), and he said this better than I possibly could.

We were talking about the choices we make, and he said that we essentially do the things we want to do. We choose everything we do every day. While it may feel like some things are not choices, we're essentially making value statements with each choice we make. We're saying that doing this is more important than that. Going to work is more important than sleeping in. Going to a family dinner is more important than a party with friends. At the end of the day, we're in control of our life and we choose what we do. Instead of thinking that things are out of your control and you don't have time or a say, own the choices you make and take control of your life. It's OK if you choose something that doesn't align with your dreams, but own it. Don't say you can't do it. Own that you're choosing not to.

If you are constantly choosing something that doesn't align with the goals you have set for yourself, it might be time to re-evaluate just how important your goals are. If you're not willing to sacrifice to make them come true, then perhaps the goals you have set aren't right for you. I'm not saying this as a negative, as self-awareness is a crucial aspect of success, but I'm saying this because you're wasting time chasing a dream that will never happen. If you can't give something up for the goals and dreams you have, you're basically holding onto a wish. Find something else to pursue, something that makes you want to sacrifice to achieve.

"If you don't sacrifice for what you want, what you want becomes the sacrifice." -Unknown

Success is very rarely about doing what we want to do right now. Ultimately, it's about making decisions based on what we want most later. Most of the time it is about making choices to do the things we have to do in order to become the thing we want to become. I think this is why success is so hard to achieve. We so often want to do the "fun" or "easy" thing, but success and greatness are very seldom fun and easy. It's a lot of focused and dedicated hard work, combined with difficult choices and sacrifice. Greatness is working out at 5 a.m. because you know the rest of the day is going to be too busy to get a workout in. It's skipping lunch with friends so you can hammer out the details of your presentation. It's dinner at the office so you can close the big deal or finish up the final details of a new product.

Nobody wants to do these things. Nobody wants to miss out on time with friends and family or wake up before the sun rises. Nobody enjoys the pain and suffering of two workouts in a day. But the vision of what they want to become and the understanding of what has to be done is greater than the choice not to do what is necessary. There's that word again: choice. It's up to you. It is your choice whether or not you become great. You can choose to do enough, or you can choose to do more. The choice is yours!

This is one of the things I wish someone would have told me growing up. I was never afraid of hard work. I talked about that earlier. I actually enjoyed work. But the idea or understanding of sacrifice was never taught to me. I think this is where I lost my way for a while. I chose the fun over the purposeful, the easy way over the right way. In college it started with going to parties and enjoying a few adult beverages. I didn't do that until my sophomore year. My freshman year I chose to sacrifice my social standing and a little fun for a life of sobriety and focus, but my sophomore and junior years I enjoyed going to parties and hanging with friends. I didn't sacrifice my time to put in more work: I just did enough.

What I learned most about this moment in my life is that my change in behavior didn't make a huge or immediate impact on my success. I'm sure some of you reading this are probably asking, "Why does it matter, then?" What I mean is there was a dropoff in my performance, but it was subtle, and if you didn't look for it you wouldn't fully know why. I went from being a First Team All-American to just an average starter. I didn't lose playing time, but I wasn't standing out the way I did the year before. The change was small and subtle, which makes it harder to recognize. This is the scary part: You may think you're still doing what you need to do to be successful, but in fact you're slowly cutting corners and losing ground. The competition sneaks up on you, and before you can make a course correction, they overtake you.

The other thing that stands out about this moment of my life is that I didn't think of the extra work as sacrificing. I loved baseball and had a dream of playing at the next level, so my extra work was just part of that dream. I never stopped wanting that for myself, but I got distracted by the lure of having fun in college. And since I didn't know I was making sacrifices when I stopped doing the extra work, I didn't think anything of it. The only way you begin to understand the sacrifices you're making is by really taking a deep look at your dreams and asking if everything you're doing helps you achieve those dreams. Without really looking hard at your routines and habits, you don't get a good idea of what you're giving up to achieve success. That's when it becomes easy to take a wrong step.

Let this story be a reminder of the importance of sacrificing for the things you want. Don't lose out on achieving a dream or a goal because you slowly stop sacrificing for that dream. If there is something that drives you each day, give it everything you have. Be willing to sacrifice now for the future you want. Ask yourself each time you do something: "Does this help me achieve my goal?" If the answer is no, remember that if you choose to do it anyway, you are doing it at the detriment of your dreams. Stay focused on what you want.

Action Steps:
It's time to take note of the things you're doing in the pursuit of excellence. Are you choosing things that support your dreams? Are you sacrificing things you

want to do now because they don't serve your long-term goals? People often hear the words "sacrifice" and "suffer" and think of extremes. Sacrificing a few drinks with friends to put in work toward your bigger goals is a sacrifice. Suffering may be something as simple as an extra 30 minutes of training/practice when you're exhausted.

Take account of your actions and routines. When was the last time you sacrificed doing something because it didn't serve your bigger goal? Are your actions in line with your dreams? Are you giving up things that hurt your goals and suffering through things you don't want to do but know will help?

For me, a simple sacrifice I made was giving up pop in high school. It doesn't seem like much, but it was not helping me achieve my athletic dreams. Nowadays I give up going out with friends and playing recreational sports to spend time working on this book and my podcast and being with my family. I suffer through workouts and the monotony of everyday tasks that need to get done in order for me to continue on my quest for excellence.

I challenge you to choose things that serve your bigger purpose and sacrifice some things you enjoy for that dream. I challenge you to suffer through doing the little things every day, even when you don't feel like it. I challenge you to embrace the suffering and honor the sacrifices in order to become more than you were yesterday. I challenge you to be great!

"I hated every minute of training. But I said, 'Don't quit. Suffer now and live the rest of your life a champion.'" -Muhammad Ali

-Build a Strong Team-

"No one achieves anything alone."
-Leslie Knope

Greatness is never achieved by accident, and it is rarely achieved alone. The people we've talked about in this book who have achieved excellence at the highest level all had a team around them. They had people who supported them, pushed them, told them the hard truth, taught them lessons, held them accountable, and assisted their growth along the way. You can do a lot of great things in this world by yourself, but to achieve the highest levels of success and excellence, you need a great team around you. I think this might be one of the more difficult things to accomplish, because who do we surround ourselves with?

The truth is we have complete control over who we choose to let influence our lives. People may show up in our lives outside of our control, but only we give them power to influence our thoughts and beliefs or our pursuit of excellence. It's important to surround yourself with a team of people who want to see you succeed. A team that believes in you and supports everything you do. Not a team that coddles you or tells you what you want to hear—that's not what I'm saying. This team should believe in you enough to tell you when they think you're wrong. Only that team will be strong enough to help you on your journey.

The support side of my team starts with my parents. My parents have supported my dreams and goals every step of my journey. They've been on my team since I was playing T-ball and peewee football, and through my college career, starting my own business, and every journey in between. While they were a constant support along my journey, they never pushed me to be something they wanted me to be. They supported my dreams by encouraging me to work harder than everyone else. They said if you work harder than those around you, anything you want to achieve is possible. It wasn't because I tried that I was going to get rewarded, it was because I worked hard that I would give myself a chance. They've always been my biggest fans and support.

I understand not everyone is lucky enough to have parents who are part of their team, but that doesn't have to stop you. While, yes, my parents have played a huge influence in my life, they are just a portion of my team. The rest of my team was entirely my choice, just as who you decide to have on your team is your choice. Each person should provide value to you and propel you closer to your dreams and goals. You don't have time for people who want to bring you down, tell you that you can't, or think maybe you're dreaming a little too big. It's time to let them go.

I've always been lucky to have good friends that shared my dream of athletic excellence. These friends would always push me to be more and achieve more. We'd practice together outside of required times, we'd work out together, and we'd talk about our dreams of playing in the MLB or NBA. We pushed each other to higher levels of athletic performance. I was lucky to have great teammates and friends who challenged me in this way. But even though these friends pushed me and challenged me, they weren't part of my team.

The first friend I had on my team was my high school best friend, Kyle Collins. The reason he was on my team then and still is to this day is because he's never once wavered in his belief in me. When everyone else wanted to go to parties or dances or football games, he stood by my side and we would go to the gym or shoot hoops. He didn't play baseball, but supported me every step of the way on my quest to be the best baseball player I could be. Two stories really stand out about our relationship and illustrate why he's always been a part of my team.

The first one is from right after I was extremely sick, which I talked about earlier. I mentioned my comeback from being extremely ill and weak to being stronger than I was before I got sick. What I didn't mention was that Kyle was with me every step of the way. He was there with me for my first day back in the gym, spotting me as I tried to bench 95 pounds. He supported me and motivated me to come back day after day, telling me I'd be back to full strength in no time. Kyle didn't have to be a part of that process. There were a hundred different things he could have been doing as a high school kid, but he chose to be by my side.

The other story about his endless support for me came after my college career had ended. I was getting in shape, thinking about going to a few tryouts that summer. I was a year removed from college but was thinking I'd give it one more shot. He joined me on the track one day just to time my 40-yard sprints. It was probably 95 degrees and there was no way he could have been enjoying the heat or being on the track, but there he was holding a stopwatch while I ran. He would shout out the times. He would encourage me to run another one. He acted as a coach in that moment, even though that wasn't his job. He did it because he was there to support me any way he could. These are the friends you need on your team.

I'm not saying our relationship never faced difficult times, because all relationships do. I knew he always wanted what was best for me, however, so no matter what the difficulties were, we always found a way to work through them. Your team isn't always going to get along. You're not always going to see eye-to-eye. Sometimes you'll fight and not want to be around each other. At the end of the day, though, you know you want them in your corner. You know you want them on your team.

"There is no such thing as a self-made man. You will reach your goals only with the help of others." -George Shinn

While I was blessed to have a number of supportive people in my life, I was also lucky to have a number of people who pushed me to be more. When I think back on my life up to this point, I can think of a number of people who truly pushed me to want and achieve more. We all need people like this in our lives who expect more from us, push us to a higher level, and don't allow us to cut corners or back down in the face of adversity. These people show up in a number of ways, but they always do the same thing: make us realize the greatness within us. We are all stronger than we believe; sometimes we just need a little kick in the pants.

The first person to give me this push was Coach Gussler, who saw something in me that I didn't see in myself. He forced me to dig deeper and challenge myself to be more. One of my favorite stories from high school involved both my coach and my parents. It was a lesson on commitment and giving your all to a team. It was a defining moment in my life and one that, had I not had the team I did, might have led me down an entirely different path. My life is what it is today because I've always had an amazing team, a team not afraid to hold me accountable and tell me no.

I've told parts of this story a few times now, but it played such a pivotal role in my life I need to revisit here. I was just finishing up my freshman basketball season, where I had led the team in points, rebounds, and steals and was a captain. I felt pretty good about my growth as a player and was looking forward to the start of my AAU traveling season. After baseball tryouts I was assigned to the JV team when most of the players my age ended up on the freshman team. During my meeting with the Coach Gussler where he told me the news that I would be playing up, I asked him if I could play AAU when it didn't conflict with baseball. He flat-out told me no, never batting an eye. I begged and pleaded with him, assuring him it wouldn't interfere with baseball and I'd be able to do both.

Coach Gussler stood his ground, saying, "This is baseball season, and during baseball season, you commit yourself to this team and this program." He said I could play as much basketball as I wanted all summer long, but during the spring he expected me to only play baseball. I was furious with his decision. I didn't want to hear his reasoning or anything. I simply nodded my head and left the room. I got home and, as I mentioned earlier, complained to my parents that I wanted to quit baseball. Thankfully, they pointed me in a better direction and I found my purpose once again.

The funny thing is, I quit playing basketball for the school my junior year and decided to focus my energy on baseball. My last two seasons were two of the best statistical years in school history and, as I've mentioned before, I got a chance to continue to play in college. I grew into a complete baseball player, a captain, and found a love for the game that I hadn't felt in a while. Imagine how different things might have been if I hadn't had a team that cared about me enough to tell me no.

Had I been given the green light to play basketball during baseball season, maybe I never would have made varsity as a freshman. Maybe I wouldn't have eventually quit basketball to become a college baseball player. If my parents would have let me quit, I probably never would have learned the value of committing myself to a team. This is one of the biggest lessons from this story for me. We always have a choice to be upset and go through the motions or to focus and commit ourselves to the task we're doing at the moment. The latter will always serve you better.

My life could have gone down a different path. Would it have been all bad? No, probably not, but I wouldn't have learned the value of commitment and follow-through. Eventually I would have been faced with another difficult situation and decision, and without this lesson, maybe I would have made the wrong choice again. Obviously, we never know if we made the right choice or if the other decision would have worked out in our favor, but I believe that this was a defining moment in my life that shaped me into who I am today.

"One is too small a number to achieve greatness. No accomplishment of real value has ever been achieved by a human being working alone." -John C. Maxwell

Fast-forward to my senior year of high school and I was now a captain and leader of my baseball team. I was an all-conference and district performer and committed to Youngstown State. I was becoming quite the baseball player and leader, but even though I had accomplished a lot over the past three years, Coach Gussler never stopped trying to teach me more. I learned another lesson from him my senior year during winter workouts.

As a senior I got out of school early, so I would always go home and relax for a bit before going back to school for practice. On this particular day I took a nap, and upon waking up I had to use the restroom. I wandered into the restroom, sat down to do my business, and upon finishing, I looked at the clock sitting on the back of the toilet. 3:20! Practice started in ten minutes and I still had to change and drive back to the school. I threw clothes on, sped over to the school, sprinted into the building and tried to join my team that was already starting warmups.

Coach had seen me come in and called me over to him. He proceeded to ask me where I was, and I owned it like a captain was supposed to. I told him I messed up and I was sorry, it wouldn't happen again. I lost track of time and it was entirely my fault. He nodded and appreciated me owning my mistake, but following warmups told everyone to get on the line. He explained that we were going to run one suicide for each minute I was late. For those of you who have never run a suicide, it's a sprint that is performed on a basketball court where you start on one baseline then have to touch the free-throw line, half-court line, opposite free-throw line, opposite baseline and return back to the start as fast as you can. I was twelve minutes late, so I knew we were in for a good amount of running.

I took my place on the baseline, but before the first suicide, Coach Gussler called me over and said, "You're going to stand here next to me." I stood next to my coach and watched as my teammates ran for my mistake. With each suicide they ran, I felt my heart break a little: I had completely let them down and they were being punished for my mistake. That's not something I was ready for. I knew I could take any punishment he wanted to dish out because it was my mistake. I was ready to run. I was not ready to watch others take my punishment (and he knew it).

After they completed their suicides, the team was instructed to go into the weight room and start the workout for the day. Coach Gussler looked at me and said, "You're the captain now. You are the leader of this team, and when you make a mistake, it doesn't just affect you. It impacts everyone. As the leader you must hold yourself to a high standard of doing things. You have to lead the way by your words and your actions, and if either don't align, you will lose your team. This punishment is to remind you that when you mess up, you don't get punished: your team does."

I completed my workout in silence. When the team returned to the field house to hit, I took my spot on the baseline and ran my twelve suicides. Everyone hitting watched as I touched each line and completed the punishment they had had to endure earlier. After finishing my last sprint, I called my teammates over and told them I would never let them down again. It was a moment I will never forget, and the impact it had on me is still with me today.

I love this story because it shows that nobody is beyond needing coaching or a team. I had been extremely successful to this point, and had I not been punished for being late, I would have gone on to have a good senior year and the team wouldn't have lost anything from it. But I would have lost. Coach Gussler taught me that to be a leader means you take more responsibility for your actions, not less. You have to have a higher standard than those around you. If I wanted to be great, I had to take ownership over my life and do things better than those around me. He took that moment to hold me accountable and teach me a life lesson about leadership. I'm forever grateful for all the life lessons he gave me.

"Find a group of people who challenge and inspire you, spend a lot of time with them, and it will change your life forever." -Amy Poehler

The greats all have a team around them. Athletes have trainers, team coaches, skill coaches, mental performance coaches, agents, advisors, and more. Business owners and entrepreneurs have board members, investors, partners, advisors, coaches, and others who help them achieve their vision. It doesn't matter who you are or what you do, you need others in your life to be on your team. You need a group willing to help you maintain the skills and attributes covered in this book. There are a lot of things that go into finding and creating excellence. Trying to do it all by yourself is a battle you will eventually lose. We often don't see when we get off course, and we need a team to pull us back.

One of the best leaders I've ever had the chance to be around is Ray Noe. When I met him, he had just become the head coach of the Pickerington Central High School baseball program. He was young and energetic, but new to being a leader. He countered this newness to leadership by surrounding himself with an incredible staff. He brought people in to help him create and build a new culture, and in the process, he turned Central into a powerhouse program in a very short time. One of my favorite things about Ray was his never-ending willingness to learn and grow.

Ray had worked with my high school coach as a JV coach before eventually finding his way to Pickerington. Upon being hired, he brought with him Coach Gussler's brother Eric. I grew up playing against Eric and we were old friends, so when I showed up one day to offer my assistance with the strength and conditioning of the team, Eric talked Ray into bringing me on staff.

The years I spent coaching with Ray and Eric were some of my favorite as a coach, and watching Ray grow year to year inspired me to want to learn more myself. I watched him evolve as a leader, and his relationship with Eric was a special one that from the outside probably looked like that of a married couple on the verge of a divorce. But they were friends who didn't hold back what needed to be said, and they each respected that and were better from their relationship. They didn't say the nice, cushy things to each other. They told each other the hard truths that force reflection, deep thought, and change.

It was my first time seeing how this relationship worked in the real world. They were constantly having powerful and passionate conversations about different things. Just when you thought they were going to come to blows, the tone would shift and you'd see them return to a cordial appearance. It took me a moment to understand this dynamic, but once I did, I saw how powerful it was for each of them. It challenged them to see things from different perspectives and to evaluate their own beliefs and thoughts regularly. It forced them both to learn, grow, adapt, and communicate better.

Ray has since gone on to get his master's from Ohio State, coach baseball at IMG Academy (a premier high school in Florida), and now is an assistant at Virginia Military Institute. He has also always been someone I can count on to give me a real answer. Watching his growth has inspired me to work more on my personal development, and his relationship with Eric has inspired me to want more real communication in my life. Too often we seek relationships with people who tell us what we want to hear or are a mirror of ourselves. The successful people in this world have friendships and relationships with people who challenge them and speak up when needed. I got to see how this type of relationship can work firsthand, and they both became better because of it.

Action Steps:

Start to find your team. Who are the people on your team? Who do you lean on for advice? Who do you lean on for additional motivation? Who do you lean on for the hard truths? Who is the glue guy/girl? The more pieces of your team you add and develop the stronger it becomes. The more complete your team, the better you'll be in every situation that comes up on your journey to success. There should be someone on your team who is capable of handling any potential situation. Your team doesn't have to be big, but it does have to be capable of accomplishing any task.

Remember, this team is being assembled to help you become the best version of yourself. Your team needs a:

- Hard truth teller
- Business advisor
- Relationship advisor
- Confidence builder
- Educator
- Storyteller
- Motivator
- Coach/mentor
- Wisdom seeker
- Teammate

There are a lot of things that need to be part of your team. This doesn't mean you need a different person for each of these roles. One person can take on several roles within your team. The important part is to have enough people around you that you can solve any problem that may arise during your journey. You should have someone you can reach out to for every situation that is bound to occur.

"If I have seen further, it is by standing on the shoulders of giants." -Isaac Newton

-Stay Great-

"Who's gonna dare to be great?" -Muhammad Ali

By now, everyone reading this book should understand that I believe everyone has the ability to be great. It should also be apparent that greatness isn't one thing but a combination of many things working together. It's a utilization of skills and traits that ultimately allow you to find and sustain greatness. Sustaining greatness is just as important as achieving it. In my experience, achieving greatness is just the beginning. Those who go down in history as some of the most influential people of our time not only achieve moments of greatness, but sustain it over the course of their career or life. That's where the work comes in. While I think you need to have all of these traits in some form to achieve greatness, there are always outliers who find a way to the top without going through the process outlined in this book. Those people find success quickly and lose it even quicker.

True greatness is achieved when it is found repeatedly or held onto for an extended period of time. Those are the people who have mastered the skills discussed in this book. They apply them all the time, not just when they're seeking a new goal, but even after they reach the mountain peak. The discipline to put in the work, set goals, and reinforce your habits after you've achieved success is vital. The journey to the top might have been only slowed by minor setbacks and adversity, but the longer you stay there, the more obstacles you'll have to overcome to hold onto your place.

Achieving success is like being a mountain climber at the top of Everest. Once you reach the peak, which is 29,029 feet above sea level, you are in the "Death Zone." The Death Zone is everything above 26,247 feet, and in this zone oxygen is so scarce that your cells start to die. You can only spend so much time in the Death Zone. Just like when you reach the top of your mountain in life, your fight doesn't stop when you reach the peak. You have to fight to stay there, and every now and then you'll have to come down for air or you'll get knocked down because you've been in the Death Zone too long. Either way, the process that got you there will have to be repeated, and oftentimes through greater adversity than you faced on the first go-round.

No matter what caused you to exit the Death Zone, the trip back in will be more challenging. Your mind will play tricks on you as you try to get back to the top. You'll face new obstacles and adversaries along the way. You'll be beaten and broken down from the previous trip into the Death Zone. The path you took the first time may no longer be available to you. In that moment you must tap into the skills from the previous chapters to determine how you will make it back to the top. It is also in this moment that you have to decide if it is worth the struggle and threat of slowly dying from lack of oxygen. Will you take the path to the top or be satisfied with having made it to the top once before?

"You must expect great things of yourself before you can do them." -Michael Jordan

Becoming great at anything requires work. It requires a lot of work. This isn't a novel concept and is generally accepted by most people. Yet for some reason, few people truly appreciate what that work looks like. There seems to be a disconnect between the work and path to success that is in our minds and the actual path we must travel. I'm not entirely sure why that is, but I know that until we accept it as truth, achieving our most high-reaching goals won't happen. There are no shortcuts to greatness, no secret doors or hidden pathways, because even if you find a way around the difficult steps to get to a certain goal, that success will be short-lived. Embrace the challenges that lie ahead and move through them with purpose and focus. Forge your own path up the mountains in your life.

To build off of the Death Zone concept I mentioned previously, I like thinking about goals, dreams, and pathways to greatness as different paths up a mountain. We all have mountains to scale in our lives. We all have things we hope to achieve and dreams we are chasing, and thinking of them as mountains to climb is the perfect metaphor. This is because mountains come in different sizes and shapes with different challenges and obstacles. Some are one-day climbs while others take multiple days. This is also true with the goals we have. The other thing about climbing a mountain is that getting to the top is only part of the journey, because once you're there you can see other mountains to climb and new journeys that you will pursue next.

When you take time to dissect the goals you have, what kind of mountain are you climbing? Is this a small, one-day climb to get you started toward a bigger goal, or is this a massive dream that will consume multiple days and years? That is going to determine how you approach your climb. We need to determine what kind of equipment and planning you will need to make your climb a success. Is there anyone else with you on this climb? How important is it that you reach this summit? What is your Why for making this climb?

While I've never taken on one of the big mountains (Annapurna, Everest, K2, Denali, etc.), I've done several smaller climbs, and climbing a mountain, no matter the size, is an incredible experience. It's an experience that challenges you to dig deep into your mind, to overcome obstacles and forge a path that sometimes has never been taken before. Even if the mountain you're climbing has been scaled a hundred times before by many different people, you must find your own path. Maybe the person who came before you was a better climber, maybe the weather wasn't as harsh for them, or maybe they had a better guide. If you only set out with the mindset that "I must follow this path" and you don't allow yourself an option to change course, you may never reach your summit. We must be willing to adapt our path and evolve our strategies when working our way up the mountain.

Take a minute and imagine that you're at base camp for your climb of Mount Everest. You're standing there looking up toward the peak, knowing that the climb ahead is going to challenge you in every possible way. There is no direct path to the summit, there is no easy way or shortcut. The only way to get there is to continue to put one foot in front of the other and to keep climbing. As you set off on your journey, a group next to you begins their climb as well. They take off fast and jump out ahead of you, charging up the mountain. In your mind you think, "I'm already falling behind and I need to speed up," but this is your climb. Don't feel that you must move at the pace of those around you.

As the climb continues, you see the group that left before you in the distance moving farther ahead. You feel the air change, which forces you to slow down even more. The climb has already taken its toll on you, and you're just in the first phase of it. Thoughts begin to bubble up: "There's no way I can do this"; "I've only just started and I can't even keep up with the other group for a day"; "Why am I doing this?" The negativity in you says it's impossible and you should quit. There's no way you have what it takes to make it.

As the thoughts of negativity push against you, you grasp at your "why." The power of your Why gives you strength to keep moving, it motivates you to continue on. Before you know it, you have a second wind and are moving quickly up the mountain.

At the end of several days, while setting up camp, the thoughts of doubt creep back in. You can no longer see the group that left at the same time you did. The peak doesn't look any closer and the path ahead looks more treacherous than anything you've faced up to this point. While you're looking up at the peak, a storm rolls in, blocking the view of your final destination. The storm erases the footsteps of those who came before you. All of a sudden your task has become even more daunting. Looking into the empty space before you, there is no end in sight and no guidelines to help you on your way. *Do I really have what it takes?* In this moment of doubt, you turn away from your goal and look back down the mountain. In the distance, what look like tiny little fleas move about at the base of the mountain and tiny lights flicker. For the first time you realize just how far you've already come and a new surge of energy fills you with hope. Sometimes we lose sight of how much we've accomplished when we're always looking at a target that lies ahead of us. Take time to appreciate everything you've accomplished on your journey.

The next day you set out again, moving toward the peak. As you begin your climb, it isn't long before you reach a part of the path that has been washed away by the storm that rolled through. For several hours you move laterally around the mountain, searching for a path to take upward. This is a part of every climb. There will come a time where you plateau or feel stuck. But remember that a plateau isn't a stopping point, it's just a time where you are searching for a new path to the summit. A storm has altered your path and it is up to you to continue to move, even if it is laterally. During your search for a path, you come across the group that left when you did. They are heading back down the mountain. "There's no way up; the storm has blocked our path," they tell you.

Disappointed, you think your journey is over. However, instead of stopping, you continue to navigate around the mountain. After a few more hours, you see a small opening that leads up the mountain. The path is very steep and not very wide, but you decide for the first time on this trip that nothing is going to stop you. The climb is hard and very slow, but you forge on with everything you have. With your head down and a steady "one foot in front of the other" mentality, you chip away at your climb. After what seems like hours, body aching and mind reeling, thoughts of quitting surface once again. This part of the trek has taken its toll on you, and you're not sure you have anything left. Slowly, you push through the thoughts and pain, one step, then another. Then, before you know it, the path widens and levels out and you find yourself upright. The clouds part and the skies open up, and you find yourself at the top.

You look out over the world around you. Everything seems so far away as you take in all you've accomplished. You did it. You made it to the top and achieved all you set out to do on your journey. As you stand there taking in your accomplishment, you see a new peak in the distance, one that looks even taller and more challenging, and the next phase of your journey is revealed. This is how the journey to greatness is, because it never ends. We are constantly striving to achieve more and become better. Once we conquer one mountain, we find a new one to climb. The learning and growing and testing ourselves never ends.

With each mountain we climb, a taller one emerges, with more obstacles and new challenges. How we look at the world around us and our willingness to take on challenges ultimately determines our final destination. Don't try to move at anyone else's pace or try to follow in someone else's footsteps. This journey is yours to take and yours alone. People will help you, and you don't have to isolate yourself from those around you, but nobody can climb for you.

Nobody can overcome the obstacles and clear the path except you. And when you feel like you can't go on, remember that you might be almost to your destination, so keep going. It is in our toughest moments that we make the greatest strides. We only fail when we quit, so keep searching for a path even when all the routes ahead seem impossible. Scale as many mountains as you can in this life, and always keep climbing.

"People do not decide to become extraordinary. They decide to accomplish extraordinary things." -Edmund Hillary

When you begin to apply the various tools and attributes from this book to your life, you will notice a shift. It may not be a big one at first, but you will notice that you start to win just a little bit more. Small daily wins over time add up to give you a chance at doing something extraordinary. The hardest thing about this pursuit is that even if you are someone who can change all of these things at once (which I don't recommend doing), there will still be a period of time where it will feel like nothing changes. This is greatness's way of testing you. Greatness wants to see if you are truly committed to becoming great or if you just like the idea of being great. Many people like the idea of being great but lack the consistency and long-term vision to stay the course and actually achieve success.

I think this is the hardest truth to swallow when it comes to greatness. If you're starting your journey today, I'll see you in fifteen to twenty years when you finally reach the top of your mountain. Sure, you may get there faster, but you may also get there slower, so I want to make sure you know what you're signing up for. This isn't some day cruise or lazy river adventure. This is a trek through rough jungle terrain and rugged wasteland. These are hard, long days, repeated over years, with a vision of what might happen.

There are no shortcuts. There is no easy way. This is something you must believe in with all of your being. You must be willing to work, sacrifice, face failure and fear, overcome adversity, hold onto belief, and be resilient, while remaining curious and constantly adapting to the changing environment. Then, and only then, you might eventually find yourself on top of the mountain you're climbing. Only then will you find steady and consistent wins that will lead you to greatness.

There's nothing glamorous about the process to greatness. Sure, once you achieve ultimate success, you might get some perks of being there, but be careful because if you enjoy them too much, you won't stay great for long. This may seem like a never-ending quest, and to some extent I believe it is. As I mentioned above, achieving greatness is part one, sustaining it is part two. That's where the real work begins and your true legacy is built. Ultimately, the level of greatness you achieve is up to you. It's up to you to decide what you're willing to do to achieve your goals and dreams.

Everyone has greatness in them, but not everyone has what it takes to unlock the door that is holding it back. The door to greatness must be opened in order to reveal what you're truly capable of. There are a few ways you can do this: find the key, pick the lock, or break down the door altogether. I don't think it matters how you get through the door because each option requires you to find a way. Ultimately, greatness is about finding a way when it seems impossible. Never give up on your belief that you'll eventually find yourself on the other side of the door. Be different from those around you. Be great.

"Take action! An inch of movement will bring you closer to your goals than a mile of intention." -Steve Maraboli

Earlier in this book I spent time talking about taking action instead of waiting for motivation. Action is an important factor in success. The ability to create movement on something allows you the possibility of creating success. Take another look at that quotation above: "An inch of movement will bring you closer to your goals than a mile of intention." How many times have you thought about doing something but never got started? Dreamed about making a change only to hesitate on taking the first step? Nothing is ever accomplished without taking action.

The idea of action came up twice recently in conversations. The first time was with a friend of mine who was talking about people at work. He said he was recently put in charge of a group and everyone kept coming to him with questions about every step they were supposed to take. The answer could be right in front of these employees and they would still ask what they were to do next. They were unable to take action. They had all the information they needed to take action, yet they were paralyzed.

This makes me think about today's students. So often they are unable to create a solution without being told what to do next. I see it all the time as a coach, too. The ability to apply knowledge is a skill too many lack today. I find it frustrating when I get asked a question by an athlete, only to discover through questioning that they already knew the answer. They just wanted me to tell them what to do next. The greats don't wait to be told what to do. The greats take risks and try things and jump into the deep end without fully knowing how to swim. Stop waiting for someone to tell you it's OK to do something: take action. Create movement and trust your decisions.

The other conversation was centered around fitness and health. We were talking about how so many people claim they want to lose weight and set goals only to continuously put them off. This isn't just a weight-loss issue. I hear stories about ideas and dreams that people have all the time during my training sessions, but nothing ever comes of it. The idea is as far as it goes. There are some amazing ideas that are never getting off the ground because we are unable to take action. Stop second-guessing your dreams and goals. Stop waiting for someone to tell you it's OK to start. Stop making excuses for why right now isn't the right time. There is no right time, there is only this time. Take action, do it now, create momentum.

There is so much information available to us today with the internet. The truth is we know a lot. And if we don't know the answer, we can almost always find it. The answer to most of our questions is at our fingertips. There is more information available to us today than ever before. Yet for some reason we are still out here looking for answers, trying to understand how we can make our dreams come true. How can we create success? By waiting for permission to try something new or by taking our next step? You have the solution you seek, and if you don't, you can find it along the way.

You can basically Google any of the chapters in this book and receive information on the topics. Want to create better habits? Google it. Want to learn about resilience? Google it. There is little about success you can't find information on. The truth is, a lot of us know what to do. But knowing what to do and doing what you have to do are two different things. Don't be a knower, be a doer. It is time to take action.

What takes most people to the next level is the decision they make to take action. Instead of talking about skipping the McDonald's line because they're trying to lose weight, they actually go home and make dinner. Instead of talking about how they want to start writing a book, they actually sit down and put some words on a page. Instead of saying they're going to make an impact, they actually go to work making a difference. The action is what starts them on the path to success. You know enough to be successful; you just have to take the leap and start treading water.

The time is now to be great. Not tomorrow, not next month, not next year. There will never be a right time, there is only this time. Make a commitment to yourself to take action. Be bold and make a decision to take the first step. It doesn't have to be a big step. It doesn't have to be multiple steps. It just has to be movement in the direction you want to go. Create momentum and watch how you start rolling. Like a ball sitting near an incline, a little push is all it takes to get it going, but once it gets moving, there is no stopping it.

"What is the point of being alive if you don't at least try to do something remarkable?" -John Green

-Thank You-

The quest for greatness is often long and lonely. I appreciate you joining me on my journey to discover greatness. I'm not there yet, but I'm closer today than I was yesterday. I think that's an important thing to remember. We may never reach the level of success of someone like Michael Jordan, Tom Brady, Steve Jobs, Jimi Hendrix, or John Wooden, but we can strive for excellence every day. I truly believe the journey toward greatness is just as important as the final destination. Even the people I listed above didn't stop pursuing excellence when they found greatness: they searched for more.

Our daily pursuit of excellence should be our judge, not where we ultimately end up. I believe if we all pursue a life of greatness, we will achieve incredible things along the way. Who's to say where we end up, but if we focus our efforts every day on being our best version and living our life with purpose and direction, we will end up being very satisfied.

I believe I have what it takes to achieve something special in this life. I believe you do as well. It is up to us to live a life filled with purpose. It is up to us to help others live with purpose as well. Our final destination is hard to see right now, but as long as you're closer to your goal next year than you are today, you are living life the right way.

Lastly, I hope you find my journey helpful. As you can see, I've had some success and some setbacks and failure along the way. My journey isn't perfect, but my difficulties allow me to appreciate the wins. I've not achieved the level of greatness that I want for myself, but I believe I'm heading in the right direction. I also hope this book inspires you to continue your quest for greatness. It's never too late to commit yourself to living a life of excellence and pursuing a passion. Don't settle for less than being great. Keep reaching for the stars. You may fall flat on your face, but remember, no matter what happens, whenever you fall, always get up.

242

To inquire about a possible appearance or coaching—please visit Charles at www.charlesaschultz.com

---

Connect with Charles
Facebook @charlesaschultz1983
Instagram @coach_schultz7

www.charlesaschultz.com